IJHAC

International Journal of Humanities and Arts Computing

A journal of digital humanities

Volume 10
(Number 1 2016)

EDITORS
David J. Bodenhamer and Paul S. Ell

Digital Methods for Complex Datasets

Guest Editors
Jennifer Guiliano and Mia Ridge

Published by Edinburgh University Press,
with the support of the
Association for History and Computing, the Electronic Cultural Atlas Initiative,
Digital Resources in the Humanities and Arts, and TELDAP.

Subscription rates for 2016

Two issues per year, published in March and October

		Tier	UK	EUR	RoW	N. America
Institutions	Print& online	1	£78.00	£85.30	£89.90	$153.00
		2	£97.50	£104.80	£109.40	$186.00
		3	£122.00	£129.30	£133.90	$227.50
		4	£146.50	£153.80	£158.40	$269.50
		5	£165.50	£172.80	£177.40	$301.50
	Online	1	£66.00	£66.00	£66.00	$112.00
		2	£82.50	£82.50	£82.50	$140.50
		3	£103.50	£103.50	£103.50	$176.00
		4	£124.00	£124.00	£124.00	$211.00
		5	£141.00	£141.00	£141.00	$239.50
	Additional print volumes		£68.00	£73.50	£80.00	$136.00
	Single issues		£53.50	£57.00	£60.00	$102.00
Individuals	Print		£37.00	£44.50	£49.00	$83.50
	Online		£37.00	£37.00	£37.00	$63.00
	Print & online		£45.50	£53.00	£57.50	$98.00
	Back issues/ single copies		£20.50	£24.00	£26.50	$45.00

How to order

Subscriptions can be accepted for complete volumes only. Print prices include packing and airmail for subscribers out with the UK. Volumes back to the year 2000 (where applicable) are included in online prices. Print back volumes will be charged at the current volume subscription rate.

All orders must be accompanied by the correct payment. You can pay by cheque in Pound Sterling or US Dollars, bank transfer, Direct Debit or Credit/Debit Card. The individual rate applies only when a subscription is paid for with a personal cheque, credit card or bank transfer.

To order using the online subscription form, please visit www.euppublishing. com/page/ijhac/subscribe

Alternatively you may place your order by telephone on +44 (0)131 650 4196, or email to journals@eup.ed.ac.uk using your Visa or Mastercard credit card. Don't forget to include the expiry date of your card, the security number (three digits on the reverse of the card) and the address that the card is registered to.

Please make your cheque payable to Edinburgh University Press Ltd. Sterling cheques must be drawn on a UK bank account.

If you would like to pay by bank transfer Direct Debit, contact us at journals@ eup.ed.ac.uk and we will provide instructions.

Advertising

Advertisements are welcomed and rates are available on request, or by consulting our website at www.euppublishing.com. Advertisers should send their enquiries to the Journals Marketing Manager at the address above.

CONTENTS

This publication is available as a book (ISBN: 9781474417426) or as a single issue or part of a subscription to *IJHAC: A Journal of Digital Humanities*, Volume 10 (ISSN: 1753-8548). Please visit www.euppublishing.com/journal/ijhac for more information.

EDITORS' NOTE

Complex systems attract considerable attention from computer and information scientists, and for good reason. Much of what concerns us in our everyday lives is in fact embedded in a complex environment filled with heterogeneous data. Mining these data has become the stock-in-trade of e-commerce giants such as Amazon and cutting-edge e-conglomerates such as Alphabet (aka Google).

The humanities and social sciences also are turning to Big Data, but as guest editors Jennifer Guiliano and Mia Ridge argue in this special issue of IJHAC, we too often have identified homogeneous datasets as targets of our mining efforts. What about datasets that cross typological boundaries? Our research questions, after all, reflect a recognition that we live in an endlessly varied world, and the way we write about problems reveals a keen understanding that context cannot be well viewed through one lens alone. Yet rarely do we create or exploit datasets that represent multiple types of data, with text mining linked to quantitative data and video or audio materials, for example.

This special issue, aptly titled Digital Methods for Complex Datasets, explores what it means to pursue research strategies that straddle data categories. Guiliano and Ridge solicited contributors who already were working in this area and who would guide us as readers and learners toward methods and techniques for addressing complex humanities and social science data. The essays range widely, from lessons learned from the pan-Canadian initiative to integrate primary and secondary materials to the need to balance data models with flexible and adaptable approaches to heterogeneous data. Authors come from a variety of disciplines and share not only their methodological lessons but also practical advice for managing deeply rooted interdisciplinary teams.

This special issue exemplifies our goals for *IJHAC*. Not only does it introduce readers to a range of important initiatives and methodological advances, it fosters a collective conversation among scholars from numerous disciples who are committed to using digital tools to provide new insights into traditional questions—and to ask new questions made possible by the use of these tools.

International Journal of Humanities and Arts Computing 10.1 (2016): v–vi
DOI: 10.3366/ijhac.2016.0153
© Edinburgh University Press 2016
www.euppublishing.com/journal/ijhac

Of course, we are flooded daily with information about new methods, new datasets, and new discoveries, but too often it comes to us as blips or fragments, known best by the specialist even when containing valuable insights for other problems. What we need is more coherence in the way we receive word of such advances, more intentionality in developing frameworks to help us understand what is important and what is ephemeral. The format of a special issue seeks to provide this larger view. In doing so we hope to stimulate a common language about the digital humanities and social sciences; without it, we will not have the conversation that forms the necessary community from which we can reimagine our world.

DJB and PSE
December 2015

NOTES ON CONTRIBUTORS

Michael L. BLACK is an Assistant Professor of English at UMass Lowell. His research addresses the cultural history of personal computing, big data, and new media. He recently served as the Associate Director for the Institute for Computing in Humanities, Arts, and Social Sciences at the University of Illinois. His work has been published in *Games and Culture* and *Digital Humanities Quarterly*. E-mail: michael_black@uml.edu

Nicole M. BROWN is a Culture and Society Postdoctoral Researcher for the National Center for Supercomputing Applications (NCSA) at the University of Illinois, Urbana-Champaign. Her research utilizes archival and computational analysis to investigate how intersections of race, class and gender influence political consumerism within social movements. E-mail: brownda1@illinois.edu

Karen FLYNN is an Associate Professor at the University of Illinois, Urbana-Champaign. She holds joint faculty appointments in the Departments of Gender and Women's Studies and African-American Studies. Her research interests include migration and travel, Black Canada, health, popular culture, feminist, Diasporic and post-colonial studies. E-mail: kcflynn@illinois.edu

Chad GAFFIELD is Professor of History and University Research Chair in Digital Scholarship at the University of Ottawa in Canada. He returned to campus in September 2014 after serving as President and CEO of the federal Social Sciences and Humanities Research Council of Canada (SSHRC) during 2006–2014. An expert on the sociocultural history of 19th- and 20th-century Canada, Gaffield has been at the forefront of efforts to develop digital technologies that expand, deepen, and facilitate research, teaching and public engagement. His scholarship focuses in particular on Canada's official languages in their changing socio-cultural, economic and demographic contexts since the early nineteenth century. A fellow of the Royal Society of Canada, he received the RSC's 2004 J.B. Tyrrell Historical Medal given for outstanding contributions

International Journal of Humanities and Arts Computing 10.1 (2016): vii–xi
DOI: 10.3366/ijhac.2016.0154
© Edinburgh University Press 2016
www.euppublishing.com/journal/ijhac

to the study of Canada. In 2011, Gaffield was awarded the international Alliance of Digital Humanities Organizations' Antonio Zampolli Prize which recognizes every three years a major research contribution. In 2015, he received a Doctor of Laws *honoris causa* from Carleton University. Gaffield received his BA (Hons) and MA from McGill University and his PhD from the University of Toronto. E-mail: gaffield@uottawa.ca

Jennifer GUILIANO received a Bachelors of Arts in English and History from Miami University (2000), a Masters of Arts in History from Miami University (2002), and a Masters of Arts (2004) in American History from the University of Illinois before completing her Ph.D. in History at the University of Illinois (2010). She currently holds a position as Assistant Professor in the Department of History and Affiliated Faculty in the Native American Studies Program at the Indiana University-Purdue University Indianapolis. She has served as a Post-Doctoral Research Assistant and Program Manager at the Institute for Computing in Humanities, Arts, and Social Sciences at the National Center for Supercomputing Applications (2008–2010) and as Associate Director of the Center for Digital Humanities (2010–2011) and Research Assistant Professor in the Department of History at the University of South Carolina. She most recently held a position as Assistant Director at the Maryland Institute for Technology in the Humanities at the University of Maryland where she also served as an adjunct instructor in the Department of History and the Digital Cultures program in the Honor's College. She is the author of *Indian Spectacle: College Mascots and the Anxiety of Modern America* (Rutger University Press, 2015) and co-author of the forthcoming 2016 work, *Getting Started in the Digital Humanities* with Simon Appleford. E-mail: guiliano@iupui.edu

Hiram KÜMPER is a professor of late medieval and early modern history at Mannheim University. Main fields of his research comprise legal history, book studies, and the history of sexualities. He has a strong interest in developing new methods of conceptual history and the history of ideas. E-mail: hiram.kuemper@uni-mannheim.de

Alison LANGMEAD is Director of the Visual Media Workshop in the Department of the History of Art and Architecture and Assistant Professor in the School of Information Sciences at the University of Pittsburgh. In her academic research, she is currently investigating the complex relationships between early-twentieth-century analog and digital information technologies. E-mail: adl40@pitt.edu

Armanda LEWIS is the inaugural Director of the Office of Educational Technology for the Faculty of Arts & Science at NYU, where she leverages existing and emerging technologies for teaching and learning. She holds a doctorate in Latin American studies from Columbia and explores digital methods within literature. E-mail: al861@nyu.edu

Ruby MENDENHALL is an Associate Professor at the University of Illinois, Urbana-Champaign. She holds joint faculty appointments in Sociology, African American Studies, Urban and Regional Planning, and Social Work. She is an affiliate at the Carl R. Woese Institute for Genomic Biology and the Institute for Computing in the Humanities, Arts and Social Sciences (I-CHASS). E-mail: rubymen@illinois.edu

Ian MILLIGAN is a digital and Canadian historian. He's currently exploring how historians can fruitfully use web archives and other large digital repositories. He is principal investigator of the Web Archives for Historical Research group, which is supported by the Social Sciences and Humanities Research Council and the Ontario Ministry of Research and Innovation. Ian also works in the area of postwar Canadian youth and labour history, which he continues to publish in. His first book, *Rebel Youth: 1960s Labour Unrest, Young Workers, and New Leftists in English Canada*, was published in 2014 by the University of British Columbia Press. It was shortlisted for the John A. Macdonald Prize in Canadian History. Ian's second peer-reviewed book, *Exploring Big Historical Data: The Historian's Macroscope*, a handbook aimed at demystifying digital methods, appeared in late 2015 with Imperial College Press. He wrote this with Shawn Graham (Carleton) and Scott Weingart (Carnegie Mellon). E-mail: i2milligan@uwaterloo.ca

Federico NANNI is a PhD Student in Science, Technology and Society at the University of Bologna. During 2015 he has been a visiting scholar at the University of Mannheim. His research interests are in the areas of computational history, web historiography and natural language processing. E-mail: federico.nanni8@unibo.it

Jessica M. OTIS is a CLIR-DLF Postdoctoral Fellow in Early Modern Data Curation at Carnegie Mellon University. She received her PhD in History and Master's in Mathematics from the University of Virginia. E-mail: jotis@andrew.cmu.edu

Simone Paolo PONZETTO is Junior professor for Semantic Web Technologies at the University of Mannheim, where he leads the Natural Language Processing and Information Retrieval group. His main research interests lie in the areas of information extraction, text understanding, and the application of knowledge-rich approaches for NLP and Semantic Web technologies. E-mail: simone@informatik.uni-mannheim.de

Mia RIDGE is a Digital Curator in the British Library's Digital Scholarship team. Mia's PhD in digital humanities (Department of History, Open University) was titled 'Making digital history: The impact of digitality on public participation and scholarly practices in historical research'. Mia has held international Fellowships at Trinity College Dublin/CENDARI (Ireland, 2014), the Polis Center Institute on 'Spatial Narrative and Deep Maps' (USA, 2012) and the Roy Rosenzweig Center for History and New Media 'One Week|One Tool' program (USA, 2013), and had short Residencies at the Powerhouse Museum (Australia, 2012) and the Cooper-Hewitt Design Museum (USA, 2012). She is Chair of the Museums Computer Group (MCG), a member of the Executive Council of the Association for Computers and the Humanities (ACH) and a convenor of the Institute of Historical Research's Digital History Seminar. Formerly Lead Web Developer at the Science Museum Group, Mia has worked internationally as a business analyst, user experience consultant and web programmer in the cultural heritage and commercial sectors. Her edited volume, 'Crowdsourcing our Cultural Heritage' (Ashgate) was published in October 2014. E-mail: mia.ridge@bl.uk

Tamsyn ROSE-STEEL is the Digital Scholarship Specialist for the Sheridan Libraries and University Museums at Johns Hopkins University, where she also held a CLIR/Mellon Postdoctoral Fellowship in Data Curation for Medieval Studies. Tamsyn gained her Ph.D. from the University of Exeter studying citation and allusion in 14th-century French motets. She currently works with JHU's Digital Library of Medieval Manuscripts to develop their online capabilities, and carries out research and teaching in fourteenth-century French music and literature. She is Principal Investigator on the project APRICOT, which is producing a pedagogical hub for teaching medieval topics. Additionally, she is Associate Editor for the complete works' edition of Guillaume de Machaut and has published articles on the medieval motet, citation, and games in medieval literary culture. E-mail: T.Rose-Steel@jhu.edu

Ece TURNATOR received her Ph.D. in Medieval (Byzantine) History from Harvard University in 2013. Her dissertation is an interpretation of 13th-century Byzantine economy through an analysis of archaeological (coins and ceramics) and textual evidence. Until September 2015, she worked as a CLIR/Mellon postdoctoral fellow at The University of Texas at Austin in medieval data curation, studying and learning about digital humanities, best practices for data curation and visualization, in addition to teaching and researching in her area of expertise. Currently, she is the Digital Humanities Coordinator at the Libraries and Lecturer in the History Department at the University of Austin at Texas. Her main research interests include world economic history and material culture. E-mail: e.turnator@austin.utexas.edu

Mark W. VAN MOER is a Senior Visualization Programmer at the National Center for Supercomputing Applications (NCSA) at the University of Illinois, Urbana-Champaign. He is interested in introducing visualization to new communities and disciplines. E-mail: mvanmoer@illinois.edu

Christopher N. WARREN is Associate Professor of English at Carnegie Mellon University. He is co-founder of the *Six Degrees of Francis Bacon* project and author of *Literature and the Law of Nations, 1580–1680*. E-mail: cnwarren@cmu.edu

Scott B. WEINGART is the Digital Humanities Specialist at Carnegie Mellon University. E-mail: scottbot@cmu.edu

Assata ZERAI is a professor of sociology at the University of Illinois. Research interests include race, class and gender in Africa and its Diaspora. Recent publications: Hypermasculinity and State Violence in Zimbabwe (2014, Africa World Press), and Intersectionality in Intentional Communities: The Struggle for Inclusive Multicultural Congregations (forthcoming, Lexington Books). E-mail: azerai@illinois.edu

Lisa D. ZILINKSI is the Research Data Specialist at Carnegie Mellon University. Research interests include data informed learning, data management principles, data policy, and information dissemination/access practices. Email: ldz@andrew.cmu.edu

THE FUTURE OF DIGITAL METHODS FOR COMPLEX DATASETS: AN INTRODUCTION

JENNIFER GUILIANO AND MIA RIDGE

Our call in early 2015 for discussions of digital methods for 'complex data' drew a range of responses, from fields of study including library and information science, informatics, literary studies, English, and computer science. This focus on methods rather than datasets, technical infrastructures, or theoretical possibilities was deliberate. Digital methods[1] like those discussed in this issue cross disciplinary boundaries, but the ways in which they are applied and the questions they serve in constructing and interrogating complex datasets potentially allow a multiplicity of insights into the possible futures of digital research. The projects discussed here, and those presented in the wider discourse within digital humanities and related fields, are crafted and constructed through the choices of disciplinary frameworks as much as technical platforms or the choice of team members.

We initiated this call as an attempt to understand where complexity intersected with the digital humanities; in their essays, authors drew on methods from fields such as new media and software studies, science and technology studies as well as the digital humanities to provide suggestions and insights into our shared disciplinary future. Initially, we drew the desire to discuss complexity from a growing body of public and scholarly material related to the 'data deluge'[2] and efforts to make sense of large volumes of digital material that needed to be parsed through computer mediation rather than human intervention.[3] This starting point for our effort was the recent work of danah boyd and Kate Crawford, Frederic Kaplan and others who have characterized 'big data' as the analysis of large or dense cultural datasets that share two primarily commonalities: 1) the effort to analyze the data is beyond the manual capabilities of individual

International Journal of Humanities and Arts Computing 10.1 (2016): 1–7
DOI: 10.3366/ijhac.2016.0155
© Edinburgh University Press 2016
www.euppublishing.com/journal/ijhac

scholars (or even teams of scholars working manually) and 2) the data is 'fundamentally networked' and 'interconnected'.[4] Yet, what struck us as we considered 'big' data was that a third commonality existed; big data in the digital humanities has most often been expressed as homogenous data where projects fall into one of three primary types: textual, visual, or audio types. Due to the dominance of datasets like those derived from the Google Books corpus or through webscraping tools that cull text or image or audio files, most big data sets in the digital humanities represent large or dense cultural datasets. Scholars use large scale textual information derived from digitized volumes or the extraction of text only from hypertextual and multimedia environments or they mine hundred or even thousands of hours of video or audio materials. Yet, rarely do scholars create datasets that integrate across typological boundaries. While they might be displayed in an integrated manner, when it comes to the processing or analysis of our data, mixed-methodology has largely existed at a case study level rather than as an integrated disciplinary methodology. We were struck by Scientific American's call in 2013 to understand how complexity might be better methodological vantage point for the exploration of 'big' data:

> To bring scientific rigor to the challenges of our time, we need to develop a deeper understanding of complexity itself. What does this mean? Complexity comes into play when there are many parts that can interact in many different ways so that the whole takes on a life of its own: it adapts and evolves in response to changing conditions... What makes a 'complex system' so vexing is that its collective characteristics cannot easily be predicted from underlying components: the whole is greater than, and often significantly different from, the sum of its parts.[5]

What if, for digital humanists, complexity was not just about the interplay of data? What if, instead, we could uncover digital methods that were particularly suited to complex datasets that straddled typological boundaries? And, importantly, what if we asked scholars to explicitly address their methods of exploring complexity? We hoped to discover not just various methods that might be used as future models for those looking to understand complex data, but also to attempt to uncover some tangible definition of what constituted a complex humanities system. Humanities datasets can be represented as fuzziness and messiness within 'found' datasets such as traditional and web archives. Often, human intervention is needed to verify the results of these computational processes, which have a habit of very quickly highlighting contradictions at the level of both object and corpora. Thus, we wondered: Are complex humanities datasets defined by their mixed composition rather than their size? Or, alternatively, is complexity potentially not about the data itself—its origins, typology, standardization, or processing—but instead about the underlying humanities question? These essays suggest how the humanities comfort with multiplicities, contingency and uncertainty in sources may lend itself to resisting the reductionism that makes technical projects easier to manage, flattening messy, human data into neat binaries. Just as any seemingly simple question might have a multiplicity of answers from many disciplines, so too might our questions about the future of digital methods for complex datasets.

We sought responses that addressed the assumptions made to define corpus of big data, and wanted to highlight scholarship that explores not just a digital methodology but one that actively, openly confronts its limitations. Could a shared digital methodological future exist? Does the divide between the disciplines of the humanities and their distinct methodological approaches predispose the digital humanities to a multiplicity of digital methodological futures? Does the digital humanities need a singular methodology for complex datasets or does the interdisciplinarity of digital humanities lend itself to a plethora of methodologies?

The articles presented in this special edition are the result of an open call that sought to answer these questions. They are united by the theme of complexity—but manifest that complexity across an unusual spectrum. We begin the double issue not with 'big' data so much as a 'big' network of scholars who seek to illustrate how a single nation might be portrayed in very complicated ways through institutional records. Chad Gaffield, in his article entitled 'From Adding to Integrating Historical Data and Analytics: Challenges and Opportunities in Capture, Collaboration and Computation' introduces readers to the Canadian Century Research Infrastructure (CCRI). The CCRI is a five-year, pan-Canadian initiative to develop a set of interrelated databases centered on the manuscripts of census records between 1911 and 1951. The dataset defines its complexity by straddling a common methodological dividing line. It seeks to integrate traditional primary and secondary archival evidence together into a single dataset. In doing so, the CCRI scholars have been developing new images of Canada that highlight both collective experience of large scale social change and the diversity and distinctiveness of those experiences in different times and places. Importantly, though, CCRI considers complexity not just as a key element of the data or its potential scholarly analysis but also as a methodological intervention of the team itself. Gaffield's article illustrates how the management of an interdisciplinary team with distinct methodological approaches can act as an expression of complexity faced by interdisciplinary, multi-institutional, cross-sectional and internationally-connected initiatives.

We then move from the complexity of dealing with large teams to the complicated nature of working with reusable scholarly objects, be they objects that exist as networked ontologies or as linked open data. In 'Towards Interoperable Network Ontologies for the Digital Humanities,' Alison Langmead, Jessica M. Otis, Christopher N. Warren, Scott B. Weingart,

3

Lisa D. Zilinksi argue that it would be imprudent to adopt a single ontological standard for all possible digital humanities projects given the 'rich particularities' of complicated, messy connections between historical people, periods, objects, and places. Using their explorations of the Early Modern period as a basis, they highlight not just the necessity of shared standards for data models but also the importance of flexibility, documentation, and adaptability. They also make an important intervention in their discussion of the importance of infrastructural work as the creation of new scholarly objects. We've paired their exploration with an essay exploring a case study in applying linked open data principles to illustrate the complex relationships contained within the three line musical notation for 13th-century French motets. Tamsyn Rose-Steel and Ece Turnator offer a preliminary analysis of the potential for scholars to publish and reuse research data that highlights how one's 'networked' complex data might actually exist outside one's own research endeavor. Importantly, they promote the importance of understanding the nature of one's own raw data by illustrating the complexity required to describe and classify the motet 'in a way that allows medievalists with different research questions to make use of the data, regardless of their particular focus.' Collectively, these two articles suggest scholars would be wise to be attentive not just to the state of their data as it exists in unprocessed form; but also that the documentation of data processing and integration either via ontological categorization or linked open data approaches can lead to valuable insights into the use and reuse of humanistic data. These essays highlight the extent to which the integration and re-use of complex datasets is less a technical problem than a matter of understanding how and why datasets were created and thereby the scholarly and informational networks in which they are embedded.

Our second pairing explores mixed-methodology offered by the disciplines of education and linguistics via two different, yet parallel case studies. In her essay, 'Modeling the Humanities: Lessons from the World of Educational Data Mining,' Armanda Lewis explores the implications of educational data modeling on humanistic data. By defining the tensions that exist between educational data modeling and learning analytics, Lewis reveals that educational data derived from administrative systems offers rich opportunities to explore the boundaries that exist between qualitative and quantitative methodologies. She argues that by levering both human agency and machine-directed techniques, educational datasets offer a useful model that would allow humanists to move beyond their continuing insistence on homogeneous datasets. Her exploration of mixed methodology is bolstered by the partnered essay, 'Semi-Supervised Textual Analysis and Historical Research Helping Each Other: Some thoughts and observations' written by Federico Nanni, Hiram Kümper and Simone Paolo Ponzetto. Nanni, Kümper and Ponzetto underscore that the retrieval, analysis, summary and visualization of data relies upon the historical questions and theories of the researcher. Offering a direct provocation to historians who they believe are overly reliant on the computational knowledge and approaches of computer scientists, Nanni, Kümper and Ponzetto engage the recent explosion of scholarship on topic modeling to argue that historians need both a greater understanding of the fundamental computational and statistical principles of topic modeling as well as an understanding of semi-supervised interventions like seeded and labeled linguistic approaches.[6] By enriching their fundamental and applied knowledge, the authors believe scholars will be better positioned to influence the next generation of digital technologies to more fully reflect their disciplinary questions. Collectively, these essays answer those who might argue that much of the data deluge can be dealt within through entirely automated intervention. Suggestively, they also argue that only through the understanding of social science and computer science methodology and models might humanists realize the full potential of their methodological future.

The impact of copyright, and, to an extent, data protection laws, on humanities research is evident in our third article pairing. The 'non-consumptive' solutions that provide mediated access to corpora make research on modern datasets possible but necessarily constrain the methods available. Our third pairing opens with an essay by Ian Milligan entitled 'Lost in the Infinite Archive: The Promise and Pitfalls of the Web Archive.' Milligan notes the potential plethora of resources available via the world world web. For scholars seeking to write contemporary (here 1990s onward) history, the blessing of over thirty-eight million potential sources is in tension with the status of the archive. It is, in Milligan's work, entirely reliant on discovery tools and knowledge of internet relationships that scholars might not have. Drawing from the large Web ARChive (WARC) files that make up Wide Web Scrapes of the Web, the metadata-intensive WAT files that provide networked contextual information, and the lifted-straight-from-the-web guerilla archives generated by groups like Archive Team, Milligan argues that the future methodology of the complex web is one lead by activist-oriented scholars who seek to design new tools to enable discovery of the cultural record. Importantly, we've paired Milligan's three case studies with the work of Michael L. Black who draws upon his experience as a researcher in nineteenth century corpora to explore the twentieth century internet. In 'The World Wide Web as Complex Data Set: Expanding the Digital Humanities into the Twentieth Century and Beyond through Internet Research', Black points out that methods used by humanists and non-commercial archives like the Internet Archive are also used by those with other, sometime nefarious intentions. As a result, working with the internet as a dataset means confronting legal and ethical issues that might be less common in formal institutional archives. Opening with the most common method for comprising web-based datasets, 'webscraping,' Black illustrate the problematic nature of data collection and analysis introduced by hypertext

5

documents being an 'assemblage of component documents.' Introducing these documents as rhizomatic (and sometimes only partially archived, particularly in early web archives), Black adapts Niels Brügger's 'web strata' to offer concrete suggestions that academic projects use the user-agent string to explain their purpose when scraping (collecting data from) web pages. Taken together, Milligan and Black suggest that not only is the obligation of research scholars to engage in creating new means of discovering the web, but it is also our responsibility to understand complex data as potentially intersecting with law and policy.

We close our special issue with one final essay that addresses the future methodology of complex data—this time via an interdisciplinary team's effort to recover the history of black women's lives. Nicole M. Brown, Ruby Mendenhall, Michael L. Black, Mark Van Moer, Assata Zerai, and Karen Flynn interrogate the ways in which computational analysis can assist with the discovery of black women's lived experience in the digitized records. They argue that computational analysis can be a deliberate methodological intervention that enables scholars to understanding corpora as socio-political entities that include some voices and exclude others, and have underlying ideologies that impose etic meanings. By deploying Black Feminist Theory in conjunction with their deployment of topic modeling and data visualization methods, the team was able to uncover the ways in which narratives are shaped and constructed over time (hundreds of years), by gaze (author), and by topic. This paper, like others in this special edition, demonstrates the value in considering the 'political aspects of knowledge creation' and the contexts in which complex datasets are constructed, in addition to documenting the scholarly interests that underlie the creation of new datasets.

Together, these essays reveal some of the compromises between modes of enquiry common in the humanities and the affordances of digital tools and sources, while highlighting the adaptability and the 'critical reflectivity' (as Black says) of researchers in the humanities. This suggests that, as new objects of study emerge, humanities scholars will adapt or create new digital methods to deal with complex datasets, however they might be constituted.

END NOTES

[1] For a preliminary exploration of what constitutes a digital method for digital humanities, please see Bernhard Rieder and Theo Röhle, 'Digital methods: Five challenges,' in *Understanding Digital Humanities*, ed. David M. Berry (New York: Palgrave MacMillian, 2012): 67–84.

[2] For various definitions and current debates regarding the 'data deluge', please see Anderson, Chris. 'The end of theory: The data deluge makes the scientific method obsolete,' in *Wired Magazine* (2008): 16–07; Hey, Anthony JG, and Anne E. Trefethen. 'The data deluge: An e-science perspective.' (2003): 809–824; Lord, Philip, et al. 'From data deluge to data

curation.' *Proceedings of the UK e-science All Hands meeting*. 2004; Faniel, Ixchel M., and Ann Zimmerman. 'Beyond the data deluge: A research agenda for large-scale data sharing and reuse.' *International Journal of Digital Curation* 6.1 (2011): 58–69; Borgman, Christine L. 'The digital future is now: A call to action for the humanities.' *Digital Humanities Quarterly* 3.4 (2009).

[3] To take one recent example, there is a rich seam of scholarship using digital methods to process the content of digitised historical newspapers. See for example, the work of Melodee Beals (http://mhbeals.com) or David A. Smith, Ryan Cordell, and Abby Mullen (http://viraltexts.org) on understanding reprinted texts in newspapers, or Katrina Navickas' 'Political Meetings Mapper' (http://politicalmeetingsmapper.co.uk) project.

[4] Frederic Kaplan, 'A map for big data research in digital humanities' in *Frontiers in Digital Humanities* 2:1. doi: 10.3389/fdigh.2015.00001. See also: danah boyd and Kate Crawford, 'Six Provocations for Big Data.' A Decade in Internet Time: Symposium on the Dynamics of the Internet and Society, September 21, 2011. http://ssrn.com/abstract=1926431; http://dx.doi.org/10.2139/ssrn.1926431; Lisa Gitelman, *Raw Data is an Oxymoron* (Cambridge, MA: MIT Press, 2013); Lorna M. Hughes, 'Digital Humanities, Big Data, and New Research Methods', Digital Music Lab: Analysing Big Music Data, (Final workshop, British Library, March 13th 2015), http://www.slideshare.net/lorna_hughes/digital-humanities-big-data-and-new-research-methods; Lev Manovich, 'Trending: the Promises and Challenges of Big Social Data', in *Debates in the Digital Humanities*, eds. Matthew Gold (Minneapolis, MN: University of Minnesota Press, 2012), 460–475; im Hitchcock, 'Academic History Writing and the Headache of Big Data', Historyonics, 30 January 2012, http://historyonics.blogspot.co.uk/2012/01/academic-history-writing-and-headache.html.

[5] Geoffrey West, 'Big Data Needs a Big Theory to Go With It,' *Scientific American*, May 1, 2013. Available from: http://www.scientificamerican.com/article/big-data-needs-big-theory/

[6] In seeded methods, a list of potential topics is provided when the software tool is run; in labelled methods the software is 'trained' with a pre-defined set of labelled data. For a broad overview of topic modelling in the digital humanities, see Elijah Meeks and Scott B. Weingart, 'The Digital Humanities Contribution to Topic Modeling', *Journal of Digital Humanities* 2, no. 1 (2012), http://journalofdigitalhumanities.org/2-1/dh-contribution-to-topic-modeling/. Topic modelling is also addressed in the final essay in this issue.

MINDSET AND GUIDELINES: INSIGHTS TO ENHANCE COLLABORATIVE, CAMPUS-WIDE, CROSS-SECTORAL DIGITAL HUMANITIES INITIATIVES

CHAD GAFFIELD

Abstract   *At the heart of the emergence and development of the Digital Humanities has been the potential to move beyond the out-dated epistemological and metaphysical dichotomies of the later 20th century including quantitative-qualitative, pure-applied, and campus-community. Despite significant steps forward, this potential has been only partially realized as illustrated by DH pioneer Edward L. Ayers' recent question, 'Does Digital Scholarship have a future?'*

As a way to think through current challenges and opportunities, this paper reflects on the building and initial use of the Canadian Century Research Infrastructure (CCRI). As one of the largest projects in the history of the social sciences and humanities, CCRI enables research on the making of modern Canada by offering complex databases that cover the first half of the twentieth century. Built by scholars from multiple disciplines from coast-to-coast and in collaboration with government agencies and the private sector, CCRI team members came to grips with key DH questions especially those faced by interdisciplinary, multi-institutional, cross-sectoral and internationally-connected initiatives. Thinking through this experience does not generate simple recipes or lessons-learned but does offer promising practices as well as new questions for future scholarly consideration.

Keywords: infrastructure, 20th century, Canadian studies, interdisciplinarity, project management, Digital Humanities

International Journal of Humanities and Arts Computing 10.1 (2016): 8–21
DOI: 10.3366/ijhac.2016.0156
© Edinburgh University Press 2016
www.euppublishing.com/journal/ijhac

INTRODUCTION

At the heart of the emergence and development of the Digital Humanities (DH) has been an individual, collective and institutional move beyond the epistemological and metaphysical dichotomies of the later 20th century. Specifically, DH calls for integrated approaches that are seamlessly disciplinary and interdisciplinary, individual and collective, campus-based and community-connected including links to the private, public and non-profit sectors. Not surprisingly, implementing such approaches has proven to be challenging for numerous reasons ranging from cultural to jurisdictional. Despite specific success stories, some leaders in the Digital Humanities community, such as Edward L. Ayers, are becoming increasingly concerned that out-dated scholarly practices and policies are proving to be stronger than the forces of substantive change.[1] Others remain hopeful that DH is the leading edge of the re-imagining of higher education in the twenty-first century.[2]

Viewed from the perspective of the early 1960s, continuing debate about the scholarly significance and meaning of digital technologies would certainly be surprising to Marshall McLuhan who, at the time, was becoming both a major scholar and leading public intellectual. In 1964, McLuhan launched a major collaborative research project 'with awesome implications' in the words of the *Globe and Mail,* Canada's leading English-language newspaper. Together with researchers in medicine, architecture, engineering, political science, psychiatry, museology, anthropology and English, this project sought to discover the 'impacts of culture and technology on each other' with a view toward developing a 'surefire method of planning the future and making a world free from large scale social mistakes.' McLuhan and his cross-campus team at the University of Toronto aimed to confront the 'failure in communications' across society 'with the aid of such sophisticated machines as the computer and the head camera' that would allow researchers 'to see what a man is really looking at, not what he thinks or says he is looking at.' One of the researchers, Daniel Cappon, a psychiatrist, anticipated that 'with a model built on the relationships between technology and culture and perceptual typology, the enhanced ability to predict and control would bring light to the darkness of the future.'[3]

In hindsight, what seems most remarkable about this project is not its prescient focus on sensory characteristics or its obvious failure to produce an ideal global village or even its revolutionary fervour. Rather, what is most remarkable is the composition of this digitally-enabled research team that included professors from diverse parts of the university in a collaborative project directly connected to the larger society. Was not the 1960s a time when disciplines reigned supreme?[4] And are we not still struggling to embrace interdisciplinarity and engaged scholarship? Indeed, while Marshall McLuhan's reputation and influence continued to grow in subsequent years, the conviction that this type

9

of research team was required to study culture-technology interactions remains aspirational more than practiced many decades later.

The good news is that, somewhat unintentionally, DH is now leading the way in taking seriously the importance of bringing together different ways of knowing in order to benefit exponentially from their distinct strengths in major research projects. As illustrated by recent winners of the international Digging into Data funding opportunity, DH initiatives often look much like McLuhan's 'awesome project' from the 1960s in their inclusion of diverse scholars and scientists. In addition, such initiatives often reach beyond campus in partnership with companies and public sector institutions. But, like the University of Toronto project in 1964, the current DH 'horizontally-connected' research collaborations may fade from memory if 'vertical' structures harness digital technologies to re-invigorate twentieth-century intellectual and institutional boundaries. This possibility or perhaps even likelihood raises an urgent question: what can we learn from experiences thus far to increase the chances of successful major DH projects especially if judged primarily by the resulting new insights to the past and present?

The potential of digitally-enabled approaches to the past is entirely dependent on how these approaches are conceived and pursued since digital methods and tools – like all technologies – derive their significance and meaning from their human context. For researchers embarking on DH projects, success depends on both mindset and practical guidelines. Special efforts must be made to deal with the complexity of the collaborative, campus-wide, cross-sectoral initiatives that are now becoming so important in DH around the world. The parts of these initiatives either in terms of individuals or material contributions cannot simply be added together; rather, they must be integrated appropriately. By sharing experiences with such efforts, we can collectively enhance the prospects for even greater success in future endeavours. Toward this end, the following discussion reflects on the building and initial use of the Canadian Century Research Infrastructure (CCRI) by highlighting one model of complex scholarly exploration. Reflecting on this experience does not generate simple recipes or lessons-learned but does offer promising practices for future scholarly consideration that are engaged with complex data, systems, and humanistic disciplines.

THE CANADIAN CENTURY RESEARCH INFRASTRUCTURE

As one of the largest research projects devoted to advancing knowledge and understanding of the human past, CCRI was constructed between 2003 and 2009.[5] It involved scholars from multiple disciplines, coast-to-coast in Canada, and in collaboration with government agencies and the private sector as well as international partners. A Steering Committee composed of Team Leaders and chaired by the Principal Investigator collectively ran the project while individual Team Leaders took responsibility for the operation of each CCRI site across Canada. In turn, one Team Leader also chaired a sub-group of Team Leaders responsible for each of the substantive components of the construction: IT, Sampling, Data Entry, Geo-referencing, and Contextual Data. A similar management structure included the full-time Project Co-ordinators who individually ran each CCRI site and collectively managed day-to-day operations. The resulting infrastructure is now enabling research on the making of modern Canada by offering systematic databases of evidence covering the first half of the twentieth century. In conceptualizing and undertaking this project, CCRI team members came to grips with key DH questions especially those faced by interdisciplinary, multi-institutional, cross-sectoral and internationally-connected initiatives.

The heart of CCRI is derived from evidence drawn from the decennial census enumerations between 1911 and 1951. During this period, a wide variety of questions (about three dozen) were posed at households throughout the country by enumerators who were trained to complete large paper schedules with the questions in columns and lines down the page for the responses of each individual. In addition to creating comprehensive data from these schedules, CCRI geo-referenced the data by digitally reconstructing the physical spaces within which the enumerations took place. GIS map layers for the entire country during the 1911–1951 period enable the location, selection, aggregation and analysis of the data both with reference to the boundaries at the time and harmonized with present-day census spatial units. Moreover, the project team built a digital corpus of documentary evidence designed to support research on the context within which the census questions were formulated, asked, and answered. This corpus of contextual data was drawn from a wide variety of sources ranging from official government documents to political debate and newspaper coverage during the first half of the twentieth century. Taken together, these components of CCRI enable research on many key features of the complex and uneven ways that Canada became a highly urbanized and industrialized country on the world stage during the course of the twentieth century.

Just as the data represented complexity, so too did the research team that included historians, sociologists, geographers, demographers, statisticians, archivists, and computer scientists as well as a Project Coordinator with a PhD in French literature and many other team members from diverse intellectual and professional backgrounds. In coming together to focus on the making of modern Canada, the project team members shared a number of defining characteristics including the fact that they all had experience with, or were interested in, the potential of sources such as census enumerations for supporting socio-cultural research. (see Figure 1) As a group, the most familiar feature of CCRI to team members was the construction of micro-data from the individual-level

11

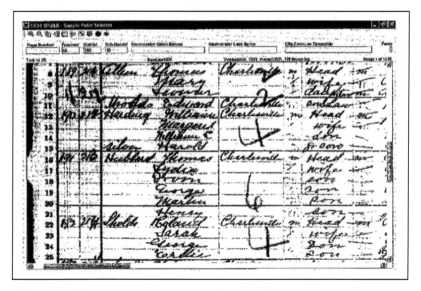

Figure 1. CCRI developed data capture software that facilitated manual selection and entry from digital versions of the millions of census enumeration forms from 1911–1951.

census enumeration schedules. Less familiar to most members (but certainly the speciality of some) was the creating of GIS map layers from documentary descriptions of enumeration units. In turn, the quite innovative CCRI component for the research team was the contextual database that intentionally bridged the traditions of 'quantitative' and 'qualitative' research. Although all of us had certainly used evidence such as newspapers and government documents, we did not have experience building a digital corpus for such material nor of systematically relating it to census data and geo-referencing within a research infrastructure.

To build CCRI, therefore, we anticipated that the most straightforward component would be the building of the micro-databases from the 1911 to 1951 census enumerations. All of us felt familiar with what was involved in such work and most of us had actually created census data in previous initiatives including pan-Canadian projects such as the Canadian Families Project that focused on the 1901 census enumeration or those related to the history of Newfoundland or Québec City or the region of Trois-Rivières.[6]

We all appreciated that many difficulties would have to be overcome in terms of the actual data capture but we did not doubt that our experience would allow us to find solutions for them in a timely fashion. For this reason, we scheduled census data capture to begin as soon as possible while we continued to think through how best to create the GIS map layers and then to build a digital corpus of contextual data.

Yet, as soon after the census data work began, we became bogged down by disagreements over how to resolve the inevitable incoherencies and inconsistencies of historical evidence that digital capture does not tolerate without human decisions. For example, what to do when a response to a census question was crossed out and replaced by another one on the manuscript enumeration schedule? The question concerned not only the interpretation of what this meant but also how to create data from both responses as verbatim evidence that should be kept as part of the CCRI census component. The CCRI team members all felt that they had developed an effective, tried-and-true, way of dealing with such issues over the course of their previous work. While agreeing that we only needed one way of doing so, we each felt that our way should be adopted given its proven success. We did not doubt that others felt the same way but we were not sure that the other proposed solutions would always work as well in the enumeration context with which we were most familiar.

While this example may seem trivial, it illustrates both the devotion of CCRI team members to the quality of the research infrastructure and to the challenge of collaborating in cases where there is a significant shared expertise that has developed in different settings. On the one hand, the overall cohesion of the team was clearly related to a common understanding of the process of creating data from census enumerations. On the other hand, this common understanding did not immediately translate into a single implementation process for CCRI. The questions were numerous. What software should be used? How should the work schedules be organized? How much training should be required for the data entry research assistants? All of us had addressed such questions in previous projects and we all had views about the best way to answer them.

At a key Team Leader meeting, we confronted what had become a significant and unexpected challenge in implementing the CCRI proposal. Discussion focused on why we were getting bogged down about the census data aspect of our work while discussions about the GIS mapping and especially the contextual data components seemed to always proceed far faster than anticipated. Before long, we admitted that we had wrongly assumed that our considerable expertise in certain aspects of the project would always facilitate implementation while the lack of precedent would complicate our decisions on other CCRI components. We realized that, in fact, the reverse was proving to be true. Unlike the email flood that resulted from questions related to census data capture, quite rapid consensus usually followed the proposal by a group of team members for the next innovative feature of CCRI.

Thereafter, our changed perspective certainly altered in positive ways how we interacted when questions arose about implementation. In practice, we began differentiating between preferences and 'showstoppers.' Henceforth, when designated CCRI sub-groups proposed ways to deal with various difficulties (following, of course, appropriate consultation), we agreed to limit further discussion to substantive problems that might result from the specific proposal; moreover, the burden was on those who had concerns to convince in a timely fashion other colleagues of the importance of the perceived 'showstopper.' In hindsight, this Team Leader meeting was crucial to the ultimate success of the project both in changing our mindset and in developing a practical way to benefit from diverse experiences with familiar research activity.

In better appreciating the implications of shared expertise for building digitally-enabled research infrastructures, we also learned the value of both-and in contrast to either-or responses to the inevitably multiple perspectives in any team. This second insight about digitally-enabled collaborative projects was not at first glance intuitively obvious since individual scholars rarely pursue multiple methodological options in undertaking research on specific sources. While in many cases, it would have been highly inefficient for CCRI to agree to implement more than one tried-and-true answer to specific questions in data construction, we also embraced the digital appetite for multiple data representations when it made sense to do so. For example, what analytic categories should be used to make sense of the thousands and thousands of discrete responses to the census questions about occupation? Rather than debate about which classification system should be preferred, discussion focussed on the various classification options that CCRI should offer to researchers based on the diverse experiences of team members.

The same spirit infused how we operated as a collaboration of both Anglophone and Francophone project members focused on historical documents that were created in either French or English (and sometimes both). The CCRI language policy called for passive bilingualism in which team members expressed themselves in the official language of their choice but were also expected to understand both languages. In keeping with the larger Canadian pattern, this meant in practice, of course, that Francophones rarely missed anything while some Anglophones relied on follow-up assistance from colleagues, particularly to grasp the nuance of certain expressions. To support this approach, selected internal documents were translated while CCRI's external communications and website were fully offered in both French and English. The ambition was not only to cultivate spontaneous collegiality within the team and engagement with others but also to ensure that CCRI benefitted during construction from both French-language and English-language scholarly traditions.

Embracing both-and approaches whenever appropriate was, of course, only a partial answer to the endless small and large questions that arose during the project. Another step forward was the development of a protocol to guide in the use of digitally-enabled communications media. In addition to the conventional modes, CCRI became the first research collaboration to use VOIP telephone lines to facilitate immediate contact between the multiple locations of the project across Canada. But we discovered that the multiplication of media, however helpful in certain respects, also caused what today we know as information overload and endless distraction. Entitled 'When Should I Pick Up the Phone?' the CCRI protocol guidelines were developed in response to the tendency to send too many emails especially in cases when they had gone beyond useful communication. The guidelines associated various types of communication needs with the various media options by specifying the type of content and audience for email messages, weekly conference calls for sub-groups, monthly virtual meetings for team leaders, periodic newsletters and, of course, face-to-face conversations including team meetings. Along the way, we learned to think explicitly about which documents or files to post and which to distribute directly to team members. In hindsight, taking seriously the challenge of internal communication helped us navigate through the inevitable obstacles along the way that required effective communication. Moreover, the protocols helped ensure that the personal and scholarly bonds among team members strengthened rather than frayed over the years.

Insights into the implications of shared expertise, both-and approaches, and communications probably relate to all collaborations, including those that include only scholars from a specific discipline. In addition, CCRI brought together a diversity of team members as well as partners beyond campus. Our collective ambition was to create a single research infrastructure that would enable research by quite different scholars posing distinct questions and addressing them with multiple methodologies. To do so, we had to build it together in anticipation of using it separately or in sub-groups. Indeed, the first major book based on CCRI entitled *The Dawn of Canada's Century: Hidden Histories* and edited by team member Gordon Darroch, includes sixteen chapters with nine written by a single author, four written by two authors and three written by three authors.[7] In contrast, CCRI itself was a thoroughly collective work. In this sense, CCRI transgressed abstract and real boundaries throughout from the initial meetings in the late 1990s to brainstorm about the possibilities of developing a funding proposal for a research infrastructure all the way to the present day when, in informal ways, former team members are still committed to next steps in building digitally-enabled research infrastructure to enable studies of the past.

The enduring solidarity of CCRI team members can be partially explained by our approach to the distinctive contributions made by sub-groups to our overall objectives. While clearly, for example, those with cartographic expertise took the lead in designing and creating our map layers, we all learned a great deal about this work and were able to engage with this sub-group in constructive ways. In turn, those involved in the geo-referencing component of CCRI were also sufficiently involved in other project activities that they not only kept informed about progress but they also contributed to discussion about them along the way. To use the words that David J. Bodenhamer, John Corrigan, and Trevor M. Harris would later use in their timely volume on *The Spatial Humanities: GIS and the Future of Humanities Scholarship*, the CCRI approach helped promote mutual learning about how 'the GIS abstractions of space, nature, and society, while posing substantial problems, are particularly relevant in the humanities where notions and representations of place, rather than of space, are primary.'[8]

This example illustrates what might be characterized as 'T-shaped' engagement between CCRI team members with the vertical axis representing a distinct expert responsibility while the horizontal axis emphasizes that such work was connected to other activities.[9] Such engagement is clearly easier in theory than in practice; to work well, special commitment is required. CCRI team members had to learn new vocabularies including additional definitions of familiar words and expressions. We had to learn about different ways of working and of sharing results. Overall, team members had to become familiar with what Michèle Lamont describes as the various 'cultural scripts' that distinguish professors on different parts of the campus.[10] Of course, there were limitations to how well we were able to fully understand the implications of the diverse scholarly traditions (or as some of the CCRI team members would say, 'scientific traditions') in our project. But the important point was that everyone appreciated that we all recognized and embraced the challenge – and that we were doing our best. Such appreciation was key to moving beyond a multi-disciplinary effort to a truly interdisciplinary engagement.

Serious commitment to understanding different 'cultural scripts' was especially needed in our partnerships beyond campus such as those with public institutions and the private sector. Two major partners were the Library and Archives of Canada (LAC) and Statistics Canada (STC), federal agencies responsible in different ways for the census. Our plan called for collaboration with LAC for the digitization of the previously microfilmed manuscript census enumerations primarily because they possessed appropriate facilities as well as expertise. One unexpected question concerned formal responsibility for the actual microfilms. At the time, they continued to be housed at STC but federal preservation policies indicated that their long-term archival preservation was the responsibility of the Library and Archives of Canada. Our initiative exposed ambiguity and, in fact, competing institutional views about when and under what conditions documents should be transferred from STC to LAC. For us, this question was irrelevant since our objective was solely the digitization of the enumerations to facilitate data creation. Nonetheless, we found ourselves at the center of debate about public policies and practices. We were therefore forced not only to learn both about them but also to think creatively and constructively about possible ways to enable the digitization.

The question of formal responsibility for the historic census microfilms related directly to what many knowledge observers feared would be an insurmountable obstacle to implementation of the CCRI initiative, the ninety-two year legislated rule for public release of actual enumerations. This confidentiality rule meant that the creation of census data for the 1911–1951 enumerations could only take place only within the context of the Statistics Act.[11] Specifically, this meant that, formally speaking, only STC staff in their role for the responsible government agency could even see the microfilms. So, the unprecedented challenge was two-fold in respecting the legislature rule: enabling the LAC to undertake the needed digitization in their state-of-the-art facilities and finding a way for the CCRI team (campus-based research assistants and professors) to create data from the resulting images for the research infrastructure.

After many meetings and draft proposals with CCRI team members working with STC, on the one hand, and then LAC, on the other, solutions were found for both digitization and data creation of documentary material within the 92-year timeframe. Special secure ways were established to temporarily pass custody of the microfilms from STC to the LAC facilities. All those individuals including CCRI team members underwent security checks (including the taking of the appropriate oath of confidentiality) to become 'deemed employees' of STC so that their work could be formally located within the Statistics Act. In addition, a virtual private network was created to connect physically and virtually secure computer 'bunkers' in the partner universities so that CCRI team members could then create census data from the digitized images. In keeping with this approach, it was agreed that the use of CCRI by researchers would have to occur in the network of secure Research Data Centres for those census data components within the ninety-two year period.[12] The 1911 and 1921 data have, therefore, now become available virtually along with all the contextual data, while the remaining components will be released publicly at the appropriate time.

Finding ways to navigate through federal public policies and institutional practices not only required learning and creatively but also stamina and good humour. Our public partners proved to be wonderful colleagues and our collective mindset allowed us to find practical solutions that even knowledgeable observers had not anticipated. But the distinct motivations played key roles in explaining this mindset. Thanks to external funding and labour, STC was able to ensure that historic census enumerations became available for study as an addition to their own focus on modern-day data. LAC saw value in collaboration with universities to produce enduring research infrastructures based on current and future archival holdings. In approaching these institutions, we had emphasized our interest in making these contributions rather than focusing on our need for digitization or the need to work within the legislative confidentiality requirements. Only after achieving a common understanding of the mutual benefit of the CCRI ambition did we address the logistical questions, however substantial, in fulfilling this ambition. This work began informally in 1999 four years before funding was awarded; its importance was evident throughout the years until the CCRI was completed in 2009.

It should be kept in mind that such collaboration can never be taken for granted even after it is well established. Changes in public sector leadership have meant that the accomplishments of CCRI require continuing attention to sustain them. Most disturbingly, neither LAC nor STC agreed to take responsibility for maintaining the digitized images of the historic census enumerations and thus they have been deleted from their archival holdings in recent years, blaming budget cuts. This decision meant that the painstaking work of CCRI team members to improve the quality of the microfilms including correcting mistakes in how manuscript pages were ordered are now lost and will require new efforts as the ninety-two-year period moves forward in time. Fortunately, both institutions continue to collaborate in many other CCRI-related ways and happily the actual research infrastructure continues to benefit from their partnership.

CONCLUSION

In his editor's preface to *Computers in the Humanities,* a collection of revised conference papers published in 1974, J.L. Mitchell observed that since humanists are 'notoriously undeterred by the mere magnitude of a given undertaking,' it was not surprising that 'since the advent of the computer, scholars have with equanimity been tackling projects which are by any standards monumental.' Citing examples like the eleven million word *Index Thomisticus* and the computer-readable three million word *Dictionary of Old English*, Mitchell emphasized that such humanities projects were 'largely cooperative enterprises' often based on 'extended collaboration among scholars from quite different disciplines.' Overall, Mitchell listed twelve distinct academic affiliations among the authors drawn from the social and natural sciences as well as the humanities. He noted one paper written by an electrical engineer as well as one by a psychologist. The expectation was that the volume would be used in the courses on computers in the humanities that 'are now found in many major American and European universities.'[13]

Taken together with Marshall McLuhan's 'awesome' project launched a decade earlier as well as other examples from the 1960s and early 1970s, J.L. Mitchell's observations contrast starkly to common assumptions today about the contrast between DH and the dominant perspectives and practice in the humanities. Those like McLuhan and Mitchell would not have predicted that, a half century later, digitally-enabled collaboration would still be the exception rather than the rule in the humanities. They would undoubtedly be surprised that collaboration across campus remains unusual. They would be disappointed that few undergraduate and graduate programs offer substantial course options in DH and those that do characteristically created them during the past fifteen years.

By focusing on the experience of CCRI in the context of other 'largely collaborative enterprises' (to use Mitchell's description), we can see some of the reasons why such work has proven to be far more challenging than expected as well as some reasons for optimism about the future. As a way to summarize the insights that appear promising for future endeavours, consider the following list:

1) If scholars in the humanities want to go quickly in pursuing digitally-enabled work, they should plan to go alone and avoid complex data. Collaboration involves human and scholarly relationships that take concerted and sustained commitment. Similarly, while no data is really simple, different kinds of evidence (as historians would say) require appropriate handling, and interrelating them multiplies the conceptual and practical complexity of their digital representation. All of this takes quality time; as we are all learning, computers offer faster ways to do certain tasks but digital scholarship has no substantive short-cuts.

2) In digitally-enabled initiatives, collaboration is first an opportunity to give rather than to receive, an opportunity to learn rather than to teach. Ask yourself first about what you are planning that might enrich the work of someone else. Then, select potential partners from among all those to whom you would like to give by identifying those who might in return give to you as well; in other words, keep foremost in mind that collaboration is about mutual benefit.

3) To benefit maximally from different ways of knowing as developed in different scholarly traditions, digitally-enabled research infrastructures in the humanities must be built collectively and interactively from initial conceptualization through construction to completion. In this work, moreover, every effort must be made to anticipate as well as possible the implications of the potentially infinite questions, perspectives and scholarly cultures that will be brought to bear by foreseeable and unanticipated researchers.

4) Similarly, special efforts must be made to collaborate effectively with partners beyond campus. Rather than a transactional approach, such collaboration should explore mutual benefit by starting with how the research community can contribute to the priorities of other potential partners. In pursuing their work, the most effective approach is co-creation in which all partners contribute both to the framing of ambitions and logistical issues and the development of ways forward.

5) In all aspects of DH initiatives, work out at the beginning or as soon as possible the rules of engagement within and beyond those

with diverse 'cultural scripts' in order to develop protocols for internal and external communications. In addition to specifying the uses of different digital media, one priority must be periodic face-to-face meetings. Common understandings about responsibility and other aspects of roles and relationships must be developed before the start of the actual collaborative activity.

Taken together with those from other DH initiatives,[14] these insights emphasize the combined importance of both mindset and guidelines. The first step is recognizing, understanding and explicitly acknowledging the complexity of collaborative, campus-wide interdisciplinary, and cross-sectoral DH initiatives. This step is necessary but not sufficient. We must then up-date the relevant policies and practices that developed in higher education around the world during the nineteenth and twentieth centuries. Such work is required, of course, not only for research endeavours but for other aspects of scholarly life. In recent years, it has been encouraging to see the efforts of the AHA and MLA as well as others such as the CHA to provide guidance to tenure and promotion committees concerning digital scholarship. Much more work is needed especially in terms of undergraduate and graduate programming to ensure that students acquire the full array of competencies now associated with humanities in the digital age. The exponential and wonderful growth of the Digital Humanities Summer Institute hosted at the University of Victoria exposes the fact that other similar learning opportunities are not proliferating elsewhere in response to the increasing demand. Indeed, one of the major benefits – if not the most important – of DH projects is the opportunity for research assistants to learn how to collaborate across intellectual, institutional and cultural boundaries. But clearly our mainstream academic programs can do more to prepare graduates for such participation not only on campus but also across the private, public and non-profit sectors. The urgency and important of such program renewal emphasizes the value of sharing insights from completed DH initiatives.

END NOTES

[1] E Ayers, 'Does Digital Scholarship Have a Future?' *EDUCAUSE Review*, Vol. 48, 4, July–August 2013: 24–26.

[2] Chad Gaffield, "New Horizons for the Study of People: Interdisciplinarity, Internationalization and Innovation in the Digital Age," in Katja Mayer, Thomas Konig, and Helga Nowotny, eds. *Horizons for Social Sciences and Humanities*, Vilnius, Lithuania: Mykolas Romeris University Publishing 2014: 153–164.

[3] 'Research Project with Awesome Implications,' *Globe and Mail* May 7, 1964. Many thanks to Geoffrey Rockwell for sharing this article with me as well as for his engagement in research on the history of computing in the humanities.

[4] Jerry A. Jacobs, *In Defense of Disciplines: Interdisciplinarity and Specialization in the Research University* Chicago: University of Chicago Press 2013 decries the increasing

calls in recent decades to break down disciplinary 'silos.' By seeing interdisciplinarity as 'part of the historical making and ongoing reshaping of modern disciplines,' Harvey J. Graff emphasizes that recent developments have multiple precedents; see *Undisciplining Knowledge: Interdisciplinarity in the Twentieth Century* Baltimore, MD: Johns Hopkins University Press 2015.

[5] From conceptualization to 2008, the head office of CCRI was at the University of Ottawa (with Chad Gaffield as Principal Investigator) along with pan-Canadian university partners at Memorial University of Newfoundland and Labrador (with Sean Cadigan as Team Leader), Université Laval (with Marc St-Hilaire as Team Leader), Université du Québec à Trois-Rivières (with Claude Bellavance and France Normand as Team Leaders), York University (with Gordon Darroch as Team Leader), University of Toronto (with Carl Amhrein and then Lorne Tepperman and Charles Jones as Team Leaders) and the University of Victoria (with Peter Baskerville and Eric Sager as Team Leaders). Leadership of CCRI was then moved to the University of Alberta under the leadership of Peter Baskerville whose often heroic efforts along with Chuck Humphrey and other colleagues continue to both ensure and increase the value of this research infrastructure domestically and internationally. For a more detailed description of the CCRI team, see 'Acknowledgements,' in Gordon Darroch, ed., *The Dawn of Canada's Century: Hidden Histories* Montreal and Kingston: McGill-Queens University Press 2014: ix–xi.

[6] For a description of the Canadian Families Project as well as diverse resulting studies, see Eric W. Sager and Peter Baskerville, eds., *Household Counts: Canadian Households and Families in 1901* Toronto: University of Toronto Press 2006. Related examples from other researchers, who joined CCRI, see Sean Cadigan, 'The Moral Economy of the Commons: Ecology and Equity in the Newfoundland Cod Fishery, 1815–1855,' *Labour-Le Travail* 43 Spring 1999: 10–42; Marc St-Hilaire, 'La géographie d'une population en movement,' *Cahiers de géographie du Québec*, 50, 141 (2006): 417–419; and Claude Bellavance, 'Les origines économiques et techniques de la nationalisation de l'électricité au Québec,' *Annales historiques de l'électricité*, Paris, France 1 (2003): 37–52.

[7] Gordon Darroch, ed., *The Dawn of Canada's Century: Hidden Histories* Montreal and Kingston: McGill-Queens University Press 2014.

[8] David J. Bodenhamer, John Corrigan, and Trevor M. Harris, eds., *The Spatial Humanities: GIS and the Future of Humanities Scholarship* Bloomington and Indianapolis:Indiana University Press 2010: 11. Also see Jane Stadler, 'Conceptualizing and Mapping Geocultural Space,' International Journal of Humanities and Arts Computing, 9, 2, 2015: 133–141.

[9] The earliest reference to this metaphor is often considered to be David Guest, "The hunt is on for the Renaissance Man of computing," in The Independent, September 17, 1991.

[10] Michèle Lamont, *How Professors Think: Inside the Curious World of Academic Judgment* Cambridge, MA: Harvard University Press 2010.

[11] The reasons why secrecy requirements were considered necessary for each census enumeration in Canada are similar to those in other countries including a fear among some respondents that their census responses would be immediately used against them for taxation or conscription or other un-stated purposes.

[12] Research Data Centres are now established on campuses across Canada; see Raymond F. Currie and Sarah Fortin, *Social Statistics Matter: A History of the Canadian RDC Network* Hamilton, ON: CRDCN-RCCDR 2015.

[13] 'Preface,' in J.L. Mitchell, ed., *Computers in the Humanities* Minneapolis: University of Minnesota Press 1974: vii–viii.

[14] See for example, the valuable discussion of two European e-Infrastructures projects, DARIAH and *EHRI* presented by Agiatis Bernardou, Panos Constantopoulos and Costis Dallas in 'An Approach to Analyzing Working Practices of Research Communities in the Humanities,' International Journal of Humanities and Arts Computing Volume 7, Issue 1–2, October 2013: 105–127.

TOWARDS INTEROPERABLE NETWORK ONTOLOGIES FOR THE DIGITAL HUMANITIES

ALISON LANGMEAD, JESSICA M. OTIS, CHRISTOPHER N. WARREN, SCOTT B. WEINGART AND LISA D. ZILINKSI[1]

Abstract   *Scholars have long been interested in networks. Networks of scholarly exchange, trade, kinship, and patronage are some of the many such longstanding subjects of study. Recent and ongoing digital humanities projects are now considering networks with fresh approaches and increasingly complex datasets. At the heart of these digital projects are 'network ontologies' — functional data models for distilling the complicated, messy connections between historical people, objects, and places. Although scholars creating network ontologies necessarily focus on different types of content, if these networks are to form a coherent body of scholarship in the future, we must work towards the creation interoperable ontological structures, rather than yet another set of competing standards.*

Here we examine the methodological considerations behind designing such interoperable ontologies, focusing primarily on the example of Early Modern historical networks. We argue that it would be infeasible to adopt a single ontological standard for all possible digital humanities projects; flexibility is essential to accommodate all subjects and objects of humanistic enquiry, from the micro-level to the longue-durée. However, we believe it possible to establish shared practices to structure these network ontologies on an ongoing basis in order to ensure their long-term interoperability.

Keywords: networks; ontologies; data modeling; historical studies; early modern studies

International Journal of Humanities and Arts Computing 10.1 (2016): 22–35
DOI: 10.3366/ijhac.2016.0157
© Edinburgh University Press 2016
www.euppublishing.com/journal/ijhac

Everything is connected, or so the aphorism goes. Therein lies much of the appeal of network studies for digital humanists. Paradoxically, however, everything is connected—except for the networks themselves. Recently, humanists have turned to network data to analyze complex historical processes and artifacts. The analysis of networks, also known as graphs, has proven especially useful for exposing and analyzing complex patterns of connection— patterns that, at the smaller scale long preferred in the humanities, had generally remained imperceptible. As Albert-László Barabási explains, 'problems become simpler and more treatable if they are represented as a graph'.[2] And yet the diverse network representations created and studied by humanists share little common ground. This essay offers an exploratory path forward to the problems of interoperability, commensurability, and shared practices for networks in digital humanities. We focus on projects pertaining to a single area of scholarship—early modern studies, encompassing the period from approximately 1450 to 1800—but we anticipate our findings will be generalizable to numerous communities within the humanities.[3] We suggest that while infrastructural work can easily be disregarded, digital humanists must create and manage network ontologies—formal naming structures of concepts, types, and relationships—that can serve as 'boundary objects', core infrastructural components for 'developing and maintaining coherence across intersecting communities' and networks.[4] To realize their full potential, in other words, networks must foster conditions for interoperability.

MOVING DISPARATE COMMUNITIES FORWARD, TOGETHER

Early modern studies has recently seen a proliferation of digital network projects. Within this relatively small field, innovative projects including *Circulation of Knowledge*, *Cultures of Knowledge*, *Itinera*, *Manner of Belonging*, *Mapping the Republic of Letters*, and *Six Degrees of Francis Bacon* all focus on interactions among historical people, objects, and/or texts.[5] As these scholarly communities stand today, however, few projects share research and documentation practices that would encourage data interoperability, understood as the 'ability of two or more datasets to be linked, combined, and processed'.[6]

Scholars in the information sciences often distinguish among four different levels at which data standardization might be implemented: data structure, data content, data value, and data interchange.[7] A data structure standard, like the Dublin Core Metadata Element Set or the Text Encoding Initiative (TEI) Guidelines, puts forward a consistent set of fields or categories of analysis to be shared across projects. A data content standard, like *Describing Archives: A Content Standard* or ISO 8601 (date and time formatting), asserts an acceptable format or syntax for the data contained within those fields. A data value standard, like the Getty's *Art and Architecture Thesaurus* or the

23

FOAF:knows:relationship vocabulary, introduces a controlled vocabulary that governs the data permissible in a field.[8] Finally, a data interchange standard is a particular technical implementation of any of these standards within a particular technology, like the Simple Dublin Core XML schema or the TEI RELAX NG schema.

Digital networks projects have yet to reach shared standards at any of these levels, and some of these differences in working practices may be for good reasons. In order for data content and value standards to be shared across communities of practice, scholars would need to agree on shared terminologies and/or a strictly-defined common means to express their data's syntax and format—a daunting and perhaps undesirable goal for humanists. We contend, therefore, that data structure and interchange standards hold the greatest potential for supporting shared practices that facilitate interoperability and commensurability among projects.[9] Ultimately, interoperable data structure standards, supported by an intelligent selection of data interchange implementations—in XML or Web Ontology Language (OWL), for example—could effectively allow for the comparison and aggregation of historical data scattered across disparate projects over space and time. In addition, it would make it computationally possible to compare the ways that different scholars have modeled similar data within their projects, creating the exciting possibility of a historiography of scholarly data models. Promoting an open, shared data structure standard for historical networks will effectively lay the groundwork for something resembling a 'network of networks'.

Interoperability has been an active area of discussion within early modern digital humanities circles for at least a decade, but these conversations have often taken place in meetings, at conferences, through grant proposals, and in the grey literature, leading to considerable repetition of labor. With this essay, we move this important and relatively long-standing conversation forward into the arena of a journal publication in an effort to advance interoperability. Publicizing this conversation has two additional benefits. Newcomers to the digital humanities should know some of the issues that long-standing members of the field have been considering for years. More pointedly, we also challenge the *de facto* subordination of infrastructural labor. By bringing this conversation into the published literature, we are arguing that the digital networks community needs to take infrastructural studies more seriously, and in a more formalized way.[10] In the following sections, we lay out some of the main challenges regarding ontologies for digital networks and propose some strategies for future interoperability.

NETWORKS AND ONTOLOGIES

Most basically, a network is a structure that includes elements that are connected and components that connect. The former are generally called nodes and the latter edges. Examples of networks include the Internet (computers connected by fiber optic cables), online social networks (individuals linked through Facebook) and air transport (airports connected by planes). Less obvious examples might be flavor networks (recipes linked by common ingredients) or networks of violence (victims who share attackers). The very diversity of these examples illustrates a core difficulty that arises as soon as we move beyond the giddy insight that everything is connected: cultures carve up the world in different ways.[11] Communities of practice have different accounts of what exists in the world and of what matters in it—in short, different ontologies. Everything may be connected, but *how*? Are people connected with one another in the same sets of ways they are connected to animals or to their physical environs? Are kinds of connections historically stable or do they change over time? Is 'everything connected' in Texas according to the same standards that 'everything is connected' in Athens, Nairobi, Sao Paulo, or Nepal? In short, what relationship ontologies are we using to connect things to one another and can those ontologies answer sufficiently to the rich particularities of time, place, and subject matter?

Since the 1960s, influential humanists including Michel Foucault have emphasized the cultural specificity—often, indeed, the incommensurability—of classificatory schemes. Humanists tend to declare expertise in a time period, a region, or a linguistic tradition, and humanist inquiry often presumes both that there are meaningful gaps between times and places and that those gaps are mostly unbridgeable. For Foucault, the unit of analysis was 'a culture', and the fundamental question was how 'a culture...establishes the *tabula* of their relationships'.[12] With classification schemas and relationship ontologies thus understood as fundamentally contingent and provisional, they have aroused considerable suspicion. The scholarly impulse over the last few decades has largely been to unmask the agendas and suppositions behind contingent ontologies rather than to add to the metaphysical clutter or to harmonize existing schemas.

Recent trends in digital humanities and information science, however, have put pressure on earlier assumptions about classification. Acknowledging the Foucauldian insight that classification can flatten particularities and formalize inequitable power relations, recent scholars have also emphasized countervailing points. There are signs of a new balance being struck. Johanna Drucker, for one, does not return to a naïve view of classificatory ontologies but neither does she treat them as merely objects of analysis. Ontologies in digital humanities have a practical thrust.[13] 'When we finally have humanist computer languages, interpretive interfaces, and information systems that can tolerate inconsistency among types of knowledge representation, classification, fluid ontologies, and navigation', Drucker writes, 'then the humanist dialogue with digital environments will have at the very least advanced beyond complete submission to the terms set by disciplines whose fundamental beliefs are antithetical to interpretation'.[14] For all its perils, thoughtful classification facilitates new questions and knowledge precisely because it groups and aggregates. Ontologies reduce the complexity of the world, but they also help us organize potentially unintelligible amounts of data into structured form. Data thereby become amenable for statistical analysis and visual display. Well-chosen categories help us analyze global attributes of networks and illuminate structures sometimes imperceptible at smaller scale. Classificatory ontologies can play an infrastructural role in linking communities, serving as 'boundary objects' that 'inhabit several communities of practice and satisfy the informational requirements of each of them'.[15] Aggregation facilitated by such boundary objects offers insights into the attributes of specific nodes and edges. Oftentimes, ontologies help us notice previously undervalued nodes and edges—or force us to acknowledge that we don't have enough data because we have not studied something deeply enough.

The conceptual structure afforded by a *tabula* of relationships also creates the conditions for scholarly communication and progress. Scientific communities have long emphasized how 'structure safeguard[s] communicability—among generations of scientists, among cultures, even among species and planets'.[16] In the context of digital humanities, relationship ontologies offer rich potential for interoperability and comparison among divergent projects and domains. Ontologies as a rule are messy and problematic, yet they are critically important for collaboration, communication, and inquiry at larger scale.

COMPLEX DATA

Before exploring shared practices which might make humanist ontologies commensurable at the structural level, we must first examine the difficulties inherent to producing the more granular data content and value standards. Specific difficulties relating to early modern dates afford useful perspective in this domain. Early modern temporal data is messy and difficult to record in a commensurable fashion between projects without hegemonically imposing ahistorical standards and losing key information about how data were originally structured. Even if we restrict ourselves to looking at temporal data associated with early modern Christian Europeans—ignoring the Jewish, Islamic, and Chinese calendars, among others—we encounter a variety of often-contradictory systems for encoding dates. The most popular calendars took months and days from the Julian calendar of the Roman Empire and reckoned the year from the birth of Christ, but disagreed on whether that year began on 1 January or 25 March. After 4 October 1582, Catholics adopted the Gregorian calendar reform and skipped ten days of the Julian calendar, leading to religiously-based disagreements on the month and the day of the year. This disjunction led to a variety of early modern responses, such as ignoring alternate calendars, recording multiple dates via fractional notation, or using abbreviations after each date to indicate adherence to the Julian 'old style' or Gregorian 'new style' calendar. This is not an exclusively early modern problem; the Julian calendar continued to be used by some nations until in the 1920s.

Many early modern people also used regnal calendars, which reckoned time from the accession of each monarch. Each kingdom had its own regnal year, with its own New Year's Day, which shifted with every new monarch. Another method of dating events is even more difficult to decipher, as it is generally non-numerical and relates instead to other events, such as 'Lady Day', 'before Michelmas', or 'my son's third birthday'. These last two cases often lead to scholars employing modifiers such as 'circa', 'before', and 'after' to indicate that any numerical date given is, at best, an educated guess. In addition, depending on the granularity of the temporal data being recorded, there are at least three further points of possible concern: canonical versus clock hours; when the day begins; and geographical variations in local time.

Temporal data is not alone in resisting content standardization; geographical data is similarly complex. When creating a database that references locations, one must again determine the desired level of granularity. For example, book historians might wish to stress the importance of specific city streets, while political historians instead work at the city, regional, or national levels. Variations in granularity leads to significant problems in aggregating data; a naïve analysis might particularize less granular data by placing city data at the city's center, however this leads to misattributions, false certainty and precision, and skewed insights. These issues are exacerbated further by issues of travel. For example, travelers might address letters from a body of water or the name of their ship. Where should a letter written in, for example, the middle of the Atlantic Ocean be coded for location? Even letters addressed from a specific port lead to uncertainty whether the letter was written in port, or only sent from it.

Zooming out might seem an appropriate solution to avoiding false certainty, with all coding at a city or even national level. However, the early modern period suffered from political unrest and ever-shifting borders. A correspondent writing from the early modern city of Mulhouse, depending on the date, may be described as writing from within the Décapole, an alliance of ten self-ruling cities within the Holy Roman Empire, or from the Swiss Confederation, also part of the Early Roman Empire, or after 1798, France. If we know no more than a regional name and an approximate date, it becomes incredibly difficult to infer anything more specific about place or time, especially algorithmically. Ignoring or accounting for the uncertainty is fine when focusing on individual instances, but provides insurmountable barriers to performing comparative analyses across one or more datasets.[17]

Such complex data choices surrounding time and geography are by no means unique to historical network ontologies, but they are still core areas to address when creating bridges between network projects. Given the cultural specificity of data choices surrounding even these apparently straightforward categories, it is unlikely that shared data content standards can be created except for the most culturally adjacent of projects. Similarly, shared data value standards for most historical data seem dubiously desirable and likely unattainable. Humanists rightly bridle when imagining a constrained vocabulary for interpreting and describing the lived environment. Data structure standards, therefore, show the most promise; indeed, even for those who might wish for a more ambitious agreement over data content standards, they form a necessary first step before any such shared data content standards can be addressed.

ENVISIONING A SHARED DATA STRUCTURE STANDARD

To envision a scope for a common data structure standard for digital historical networks, we must begin by considering the varying treatments of nodes and edges: different historical networks projects ask the available textual, pictorial, and material culture to play different roles. In some projects, material objects such as letters are evidence for nodes and edges, while in others such objects function as active historical participants in the networks—as nodes in their own right. As materials slip and slide between serving as 'source material' and serving as agents in the network itself, it becomes clear that the work these objects do must be made explicit.[18] In projects such as *Mapping the Republic of Letters* (*Letters*) or *Six Degrees of Francis Bacon* (*Six Degrees*), historical social networks are generated by means of inferential reconstruction. *Letters* infers a social network from correspondence metadata, rather than a reading of the text itself. A connection is drawn between author and addressee, regardless of whether the addressee ever receives the letter, and agnostic to whether the letter is bureaucratic, familial, scholarly, or antagonistic. By contrast, *Six Degrees*, to which several of us contribute, computationally analyzes text from the *Oxford Dictionary of National Biography* (*ODNB*) to infer social ties between historical actors.[19] Both projects collapse evidence into inference, constructing social networks which aim to move beyond statements about evidence to statements about the past, albeit contingently. While these projects approach their task of inference through different computational means, they both work with large data sets to reconstruct broader historical networks of interactivity than have heretofore been possible.

Historical objects themselves can also take on the role of an agent in these networks, as is the case for *Itinera*, managed by another contributor. *Itinera* represents modeled data about historical people, objects, and sites, but instead of extracting this information computationally, it is culled from existing sources by hand. This approach is capable of encoding varieties of inter-agent relationships currently opaque to computational methods (i.e. that are not

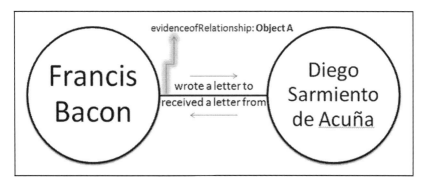

Figure 1. Basic network dyad demonstrating the role of a text as an attribute of the edge.

necessarily contained by the linguistic data of the texts or even the visual data of the images), but the process is painstaking and allows for smaller-scale network analyses. For example, by capturing the material culture historians use as their sources, *Itinera* can assert inter-agent relationships such as 'painter of/painted by', a relationship that connects a painter to both the subject of the painted representation as well as the *physical painting itself*. By taking advantage of human interpretive strengths, cultural objects can take their place as nodes in the network in their own right.

That said, texts as material agents are never truly erased from the networks produced by *Six Degrees* and *Letters*, even as the focus of those projects remains the texts' content rather than their physical agency. These texts persist as attributes of both the nodes and the edges, that is as 'source information', or the evidence for asserting the existence of any given node or the shape of any given relationship (see Figure 1). But once allowing for an object of material culture—whether a text, image, or other material object—to serve as an attribute of an edge (such as 'source'), the edges represented within historical social networks should be then able to bear any number of attributes. For example, the experienced reality that relationships are bidirectional and often time-delimited also demonstrates the need for either repeatable edge attributes (as in *Six Degrees*) or repeatable edges themselves (as in *Itinera*). Objects can be owned by multiple people, but they can also be possessed by the same person/agent multiple times over the course of time. Some relationships are for life (biological parent/child), while others begin during life and end at death (member of a group/has as member). Others have indeterminate edges both in extent and in time (friend of/enemy of), and may vary by the perspective of different historical agents. Both nodes and edges must be allowed develop their own ontologies.

Table 1. Two different edge attribute structures, *Itinera's* allowing for multiple edges between two nodes and *Six Degrees'* allowing for repeatable attributes for each edge between nodes.

Itinera	Six Degrees of Francis Bacon
Relationship type (Node A to Node B)	Relationship types (Node A to Node B)
Relationship type (Node B to Node A)	Relationship inverses (Node B to Node A)
Indexing date (machine-readable)	Relationship dates (one global and one for each relationship type)
Display date (human-readable)	Date types (one for each relationship date)
Documentation strength	Certainty estimates (one global and one for each relationship type)
Source information	Citations (one global and one for each relationship type)
General notes	User Annotations
	Other metadata fields related to crowdsourcing

But what would the structure of such ontologies be for the purposes of these shared practices? In Table 1 we take the example of an edge ontology, and present the categories that *Itinera* and *Six Degrees* use to define their relationships. Both assume the ability to add singular or multiple relationship types, dates, citational attributes, and free-form notes, albeit with currently significant differences. *Six Degrees'* bidirectional relationship types are implemented as dyads—with unidirectional relationships always paired with their inverses, such as *parent of* and *child of*—whereas *Itinera* can support bidirectional and unidirectional relationships. Date structures also vary; *Six Degrees* supports a variety of date fields with predetermined modifiers to support fuzzy data while *Itinera* has both a 'human-readable' display date field to provide the cataloguers the opportunity to express the full human-comprehensible complexity of a date range along with a 'machine-readable' indexing date field that supports search queries. *Itinera*'s documentation strength value is a human-assigned measure of a cataloguer's confidence, whereas *Six Degrees* uses a combination of probabilistic statistics and human-assigned measures. The source information fields of both projects allow each asserted relationship to be assigned as many pieces of supporting evidence as are known or extant. Other possible edge characteristics to be considered for the shared practices may include metadata surrounding data collection and/or a relationship directionality designation such as MAN (mutual-asymmetric-null); this latter designation would allow scholars to assert whether the edge between two nodes represents a bidirectional (mutual) relationship, unidirectional (asymmetric) relationship, or even a proactive assertion of no relationship whatsoever (null). While these ontologies are themselves complex and contingent, grounded in scholarly traditions, their structures are not as impossibly disparate as data content or value standards. Indeed, they are similar enough to indicate that data structure standards are the logical place to begin discussing interoperability.

TOWARDS INTEROPERABILITY

Given the complexity of the information that could inform the construction of any specific network, the goal of interoperability might appear foreboding. However, at the most basic structural level, moving toward interoperability can begin with the creation of a set of unique resource identifiers (URIs) for three types of data-in-common (in addition to an URI for the overall network project). These three broad types are:

1. named entities/nodes
2. relationships/edges and
3. project-specific vocabulary terms

With only these three classes of URIs, we thus have (1) a system of named entities which can take attributes defined by individual projects; (2) a series of relationships which can also take attributes based on individual project needs; and (3) a set of controlled vocabulary lists which, themselves, can be interconnected with related terms.

We recognize that these structural URIs are the foundation, but not the complete solution, for the mapping of data from one network ontology to another. Correlating the use of particular data values will remain problematic. Mapping named entities between projects is generally a straightforward—albeit often labor-intensive—exercise in determining which of a project's named objects exist in the other project, then associating the relevant data via URIs. This is easiest in the case where two projects already share a set of identifiers—such as *Six Degrees*, which maintains a mapping of its own URIs for person-nodes to the *ODNB*'s URIs for biographical subjects, which are in turn also used by Wikipedia to relate its own articles back to the *ODNB*. Once named entities have been mapped between projects, their relationships can easily be mapped.

Difficulties arise, however, in mapping the ontological properties of named entities and relationships between projects that do not share a domain-specific set of identifiers. For example, an early modern relationship ontology cannot easily map onto the popular contemporary FOAF:knows:relationship vocabulary, as the latter does not allow for religiously-defined relationships such as 'parishioner of', 'confessor of', and 'godparent of'.[20] Erring on the side of caution, we might map such relationships to the broadest possible relationship category—'has met'—but this does not accurately describe, for example, a long-distance godparent relationship. A great deal of information would be lost in such a reductive mapping; for example, neither sexual partnerships nor the

31

Table 2. Mapping relationship type value standards constructed for different cultures.

Six Degrees of Francis Bacon (16th–17th c. Britain)	Manner of Belonging (18th c. Britain)	Itinera (18th–19th c. Europe)	FOAF:knows:relationship (21st c. Anglophone World)
Friend of	friendOf	–	Friend Of
Acquaintance of	acquaintanceOf	acquaintance of	Acquaintance of
Acquaintance of	acquaintanceOf	travel companion of	Acquaintance of
Spouse of	spouseOf	spouse of	Life Partner Of
Sexual Partner of	–	–	Has Met
Client of	hasPatron	contracted by/client of	Has Met
Parishioner of	–	–	Has Met
Apprentice of	apprenticeOf	apprentice to	Apprentice To
Mentee/Student of	studentOf	student of	Apprentice To
Mentee/Student of	hasMentor	school of	Apprentice To
–	–	was created by (object)	–

priest/parishioner relationship are equivalent to the patron/client relationship (see Table 2). Similarly, a project like *Letters* requires greater granularity of correspondence relationships—broken down by correspondence subjects—than a project like *Itinera*, which instead requires a relationship vocabulary that maps between any combination of people and objects. The process of successfully mapping network projects to encourage interoperability thus becomes dependent, in practice, on the ability to map the complex system of data values used by digital historical networks.

Despite the difficulties that arise when attempting to map ontological properties onto one another, projects can take steps to facilitate interoperability. Most importantly, each project should clearly define every part of its data model, from its structure to the vocabulary it has constructed, in terms that are clear to their own community as well as to other scholars who may come to it from other fields. For example, the FOAF:knows:relationship vocabulary's definition of 'Apprentice To' as 'A property representing a person to whom this person serves as a trusted counselor or teacher' makes clear that this property includes several different relationship types that are differentiated by *Six Degrees* and *Manner of Belonging (MOB)*'s ontologies: student/teacher relationships, mentor/mentee relationships, as well as legal apprenticeship relationships (see Table 2).[21] Furthermore, making clearly-defined, project-level data dictionaries and vocabularies publicly available would support cross-ontology mappings by putting the infrastructure in place to create crosswalks—tables that show equivalent fields in different vocabularies—between any two projects, as need and interest arises. The creation and eventual accrual of multiple crosswalks will not only generate greater potential for network interoperability between disparate network projects, it will also support the eventual historiographic study of the data models themselves.

Beyond the individual project level, we believe the wider community of practice needs to construct a peer-reviewed, open, online resource for historical network ontologies. What we propose is the creation of a computational 'network of networks' to help scholars consider not only the messy data they deal with every day, but also the messy structures they create to corral that data into pens. The end result would illustrate how a boundary object, such as a community-based data structure standard, can itself institute a relation. In the resulting network of networks, each network project would be its own node and the edges would be ontology crosswalks. Similarities and differences between the networks could then generate new scholarly questions. We would begin this work with examples drawn, as here, from the early modern period, but assume that work would eventually be done to promote diachronic and 'diaspatial' studies. And, if it proved to be the case that the shared practices created for early modern Europe are not at all generalizable to other times and places, we would consider this a critical finding.

A peer-reviewed, open, online resource for historical network ontologies would inhabit the same universe as other digital scholarly objects, such as ORBIS or Virtual Paul's Cross, which exist because there are certain types of scholarship for which traditional academic publications are inadequate containers.[22] Such a resource would facilitate the creation and connection of ontologies, and it would further challenge the subordination of infrastructural labor by treating such boundary objects as scholarly contributions in their own right. At a minimum, to ensure interoperability it would need to contain:

- A network of digital humanities network projects.
- Example data sets from existing projects.
- Data dictionaries (at the structural level) for the example data sets.
- Detailed vocabulary definitions for the example data sets.
- Example crosswalks between presented data sets.
- Simplest, mutually-agreed-upon Linked Open Data structure standard expressed in a variety of current standard languages.

Desirable further content includes:

- Interpretation of field types, data content standards, etc.
- Comparisons between different projects' treatments of uncertainty.
- Best practices for sourcing information within ontologies.

Actually performing the work of creating a network of early modern projects that could then be expanded into the larger humanities solar system is beyond the initial scope of even this larger project. However, we have argued that taking this path is both possible and desirable—even necessary—for the digital humanities to reach its fullest potential. Ontologies lie at the heart of digital network projects and their complexities present a significant—but not insurmountable—challenge to establishing shared practices that facilitate network interoperability.

END NOTES

[1] This article was collaboratively written, building on discussions that took place during the Fall 2015 workshop organized by A. Langmead, C. Warren, and D. Armstrong, 'Network ontologies in the early modern world', http://networkontologies.org, last accessed 30 July 2015. Author order is alphabetical.

[2] A-L. Barabási, *Network science* (Cambridge, 2016). http://barabasi.com/networksciencebook/content/book_chapter_2.pdf, last accessed 30 July 2015.

[3] In addition to being of particular interest to the authors, the early modern period also has a sizable body of work on historical networks. Recent essays and collections include R. Ahnert and S. Ahnert, 'Protestant letter networks in the reign of Mary I: a quantitative approach', *ELH* 82, no. 11 (2015), 1–34; P. Arblaster, 'Posts, newsletters, newspapers: England in a European system of communications', in J. Raymond, ed., *News networks in seventeenth century Britain and Europe* (London, 2006), 19–34; I.W. Archer, 'Social networks in Restoration London: the evidence from Samuel Pepys's diary', in A. Shepard and P. Withington, eds., *Communities in early modern England: networks, place, rhetoric* (Manchester, 2000), 76–94; J. Daybell. 'Gender, politics and diplomacy: women, news and intelligence networks in Elizabethan England', in R. Adams and R. Cox, eds., *Diplomacy and early modern culture* (New York, 2010), 101–19; A. Herbert, *Female alliances: gender, identity, and friendship in early modern Britain* (New Haven, 2014); J.F. Padgett and C.K. Ansell, 'Robust action and the rise of the Medici, 1400–1434', *American Journal of Sociology* 98, no. 6 (May 1, 1993), 1259–1319. doi:10.2307/2781822; and A. Shepard and P. Withington, eds. *Communities in early modern England: networks, place, rhetoric* (Manchester, 2000).

[4] G. C. Bowker and S. L. Starr, *Sorting things out: classification and its consequences*, (Cambridge, MA, 2000), 297.

[5] *Circulation of knowledge*, http://ckcc.huygens.knaw.nl; *Cultures of knowledge*, http://www.culturesofknowledge.org; *Itinera*, https://itinera.pitt.edu; *Manner of belonging*, http://projects.iq.harvard.edu/johnson; *Mapping the republic of letters,* http://republicofletters.stanford.edu; *Six degrees of Francis Bacon,* http://sixdegreesoffrancisbacon.com, last accessed 30 July 2015.

[6] M. Janssen, E. Estevez, and T. Janowski, 'Interoperability in big, open, and linked data–organizational maturity, capabilities, and data portfolios', *Computer* 47, no. 10 (October 2014), 44–49. Interoperability can further be described as inter-connecting 'assets by publishing, sharing, and linking data and processes'. L. C. Pouchard et al., 'A linked science investigation: enhancing climate change data discovery with semantic technologies', *Earth Science Informatics* 6, no. 3 (September 2013), 175–85. Cited here at 175.

[7] For more see A. J. Gilliland, 'Setting the Stage', in M. Baca, ed., *Introduction to metadata*, 3rd online ed. [e-book] (Los Angeles, CA, 2008) http://www.getty.edu/research/publications/electronic_publications/intrometadata/setting.html, last accessed 30 July 2015.

[8] On the advantages and disadvantages of controlled vocabularies in humanist projects, see D. Shore, 'On categories of relations in networks: or, most abstract blog post title ever?' *Six Degrees of Francis Bacon Blog* (21 August 2014), http://6dfb.tumblr.com/post/95378633456/on-categories-of-relations-in-networks-or-most, last accessed 30 July 2015.

9   For example, see M. C. Pattuelli, 'Mapping people-centered properties for linked open data', *Knowledge Organization* 38, no. 4 (1 January 2011), 352–59.

10 This goal is shared by the current COST Action—'Reassembling the Republic of Letters, 1500–1800'—funded to create pan-European data on the Republic of Letters and support integration of scholarly knowledge more generally. This work is vital and we hope our paper contributes to the scholarly discussion in a formal way that will be accessible beyond individual scholarly communities and to the humanities more broadly. *COST action IS1310*, http://www.cost.eu/COST_Actions/isch/Actions/IS1310; *Reassembling the republic of letters*, http://www.republicofletters.net, last accessed 30 July 2015.

11 E. Zerubavel, *The fine line: making distinctions in everyday life* (New York, 1991).

12 M. Foucault, *The order of things: an archaeology of the human sciences* (New York, 1970), xxiv.

13 M. Pasin and J. Bradley, 'Factoid-based prosopography and computer ontologies: towards an integrated approach', *Digital Scholarship in the Humanities* 30, no. 1 (1 April 2015).

14 J. Drucker, *Graphesis: visual forms of knowledge production* (Cambridge, MA, 2014), 178. See further T. Underwood, *Why literary periods mattered: historical contrast and the prestige of English studies* (Stanford, CA, 2013); J. Guldi and D. Armitage, *The History Manifesto* (Cambridge, 2014); B. Nowviskie, 'Digital Humanities in the Anthropocene', *Digital Scholarship in the Humanities*, (9 April 2015); M. Posner, 'What's next: the radical, unrealized potential of digital humanities', *Miriam Posner's Blog* (27 July 2015), http://miriamposner.com/blog/whats-next-the-radical-unrealized-potential-of-digital-humanities/; M. D. Lincoln, 'A radical, useable data model', *Matthew Lincoln* (25 July 2015), http://matthewlincoln.net/2015/07/25/a-radical-useable-data-model.html, last accessed 30 July 2015.

15 Bowker and Starr, *Sorting things out*, 297.

16 L. Daston and P. Galison, *Objectivity* (Cambridge, MA, 2007), 295.

17 This is an area of active research in GIS, data science, and digital humanities. See for example, S. Jänicke and D. J. Wrisley, 'Visualizing uncertainty: how to use the fuzzy data of 550 medieval texts?' http://dh2013.unl.edu/abstracts/ab-158.html, last accessed 30 July 2015.

18 For a classic statement of the importance of material culture to the construction of human social systems, see J. Law, 'Notes on the theory of the actor-network: ordering, strategy, and heterogeneity', *Systems Practice* 5, no. 4 (1992), 379–393. See also, J. Bennett, *Vibrant matter: a political ecology of things* (Durham, NC, 2010).

19 C. Warren et al., 'Six degrees of Francis Bacon: a statistical method for reconstructing large historical social networks', (under review).

20 I. Davis and E. Vitiello Jr., *Relationship ontology*, http://vocab.org/relationship/.html, last accessed 30 July 2015. See further M. Graves, A. Constabaris, and D. Brickley, 'FOAF: connecting people on the semantic web', *Cataloging & Classification Quarterly* 43, no. 3–4 (2007), 191–202.

21 Davis and Vitiello, *Relationship ontology*, http://purl.org/vocab/relationship/apprenticeTo, last accessed 30 July 2015.

22 *ORBIS: the Stanford geospatial network model of the Roman world*, http://orbis.stanford.edu; *Virtual Paul's Cross: a digital recreation of John Donne's Gunpowder Day sermon*, http://vpcp.chass.ncsu.edu/, last accessed 30 July 2015.

MEDIEVAL MUSIC IN LINKED OPEN DATA: A CASE STUDY ON LINKING MEDIEVAL MOTETS[1]

TAMSYN ROSE-STEEL AND ECE TURNATOR

Abstract   In Fall 2013, the Council on Library and Information Resources (CLIR), funded by the Andrew W. Mellon Foundation, engaged five postdoctoral fellows placed in five different institutions to explore issues related to data curation for medieval studies. In May 2015, these fellows convened a two-day workshop on the sharing and publishing of Linked Open Data (LOD). Funded by a CLIR/Mellon microgrant, the workshop brought together librarians, technologists, and scholars to brainstorm on the challenges posed to medievalists in sharing data on digital platforms.[2] The workshop offered a forum in which to discuss the complexity of medieval data and the challenges of sharing and publishing it. It enabled participants to appreciate LOD's potential to express complicated data sets in our area of study and aid the navigation of those data sets, as well as understand how LOD can facilitate scholars to share and publish research outcomes more effectively.

In this article, we take the lessons learned from the workshop and apply them to a set of complex data: 13th-century French motets, short pieces of music usually consisting of three lines and incorporating manifold connections and references. Following an outline of LOD, a detailed explanation of the motet and the manner of its composition will set the scene for elucidating the levels of complexity to be found in motet metadata, and hence why the LOD model can aid us in negotiating the data. We will then demonstrate an effective application of LOD by proposing a proof-of-concept system for organizing a select set of motets.

Keywords: Linked Open Data, digital humanities, medieval, motet, music, French, Montpellier Codex, thirteenth century

International Journal of Humanities and Arts Computing 10.1 (2016): 36–50
DOI: 10.3366/ijhac.2016.0158
© Edinburgh University Press 2016
www.euppublishing.com/journal/ijhac

LOD is a web-based technology that aims to link data openly available on the web to other such data.[3] It is founded on the principle of creating and linking open, structured data in non-proprietary formats, defined and made accessible online via Unique Resource Identifiers (URIs).[4] LOD transforms information into a machine-readable format for computers, to structure descriptions and interconnections (i.e. the relevant metadata) among the multifaceted objects of information on the web. In a broad sense, the web itself becomes a publication platform and LOD the technology that gives it a structure, enabling connections between those objects.[5] LOD has the potential to transform 'isolated pieces of humanities scholarship into networks of knowledge, ultimately enabling new forms of research, contextualization, and sharing to emerge'.[6] In this paper, we provide a preliminary analysis of the potential for scholars to publish and reuse research data using LOD, via a specific test case on motet-related data.

THE MOTET

The motet emerged from a sacred setting, but was often secular in nature, though it maintained both its secular and sacred allegiances in terms of its content. These compositions were based on extracts from liturgical music, adapted to create a new genre.[7] Snippets from monophonic vocal lines of sacred music, called plainchant, were layered with new lines of music, usually bearing secular text, to create a multi-line—or polyphonic—structure that simultaneously embraced religious and non-religious textual and musical traditions.[8] These creations, often intellectual and witty, enabled innovative juxtapositions of ideas that may initially have seemed contradictory, but which allowed for a rich seam of interpretation.[9]

Describing how a motet is composed, even to the musically initiated, can be difficult. Medieval writers and theorists themselves found the task a tricky one, but it is this very complexity that makes the motet an ideal case study for the possible benefits of using LOD in medieval musicology. One of the early attempts to describe the motet comes to us from the thirteenth century, when Johannes de Grocheio visited Paris and endeavoured to chronicle the city's musical scene.[10] Likely not an expert in composition himself, Grocheio portrayed the motet as 'music assembled from numerous elements, having numerous poetic texts or a multifarious structure of syllables, according together at every point'.[11] These 'numerous elements' are the individual lines of music, while 'numerous poetic texts' clarifies that each of these musical lines has its own poetic text, and 'according together' signifies that the musical lines sound simultaneously in accordance with the rules of harmony and rhythm. In other words, this is a polyphonic, multi-texted piece of music.

Figure 1. score of motet 'Trop sovent me dueil / Brunete a qui j'ai mon cuer done / In seculum'.

Grocheio went on to explain that the individual lines are known as the *tenor*, *motetus*, *triplum*, and *quadruplum*. The *tenor* is the lowest musical line, with the other three lines higher in pitch and usually containing more notes, with the result they move more swiftly than the *tenor*. Often, the *motetus*, *triplum*, and *quadruplum* are successively higher in pitch and contain more notes (hence the *quadruplum* is frequently the highest in pitch and fastest moving of the lines in a four-part motet).

Thirteenth-century motets could have two, three, or four lines. For our purposes here, we are focusing exclusively on three-part motets, i.e. motets only composed of three lines: *tenor*, *motetus*, and *triplum*. An examination of the motet 'Trop sovent me dueil / Brunete a qui j'ai mon cuer done / IN SECULUM' will show more clearly the structure of one of these pieces.

This entire piece, shown in Figure 1, is very short. In modern notation (as it is here) it is only twelve bars long, and when sung, would last around half a minute.

In this motet, the *tenor* line (A) is taken from a piece of plainchant entitled 'Hec dies'. The full text of 'Hec dies' is as follows:

Hec dies, quam fecit Dominus: exultemus, et letemur in ea. Confitemini Domino, quoniam bonus: quoniam **in seculum** *misericordia ejus.*

This is the day which the Lord hath made: let us be glad and rejoice therein. Give praise to the Lord, for he is good: for his mercy endureth **for ever**.[12]

The music for 'Hec dies' can be found in Figure 2. From this chant, only a small section is employed as the motet's *tenor* line, namely the section texted

38

Figure 2. Score of plainchant 'Hec dies'.

'in seculum' (marked in bold in the above text and demarcated with a box in Figure 2). The segment of the chant melody to which 'in seculum' is sung is repurposed as the motet's foundational line by organizing it into a repeated rhythmic structure. 'In seculum' is indicated in the manuscript witnesses as the source of the chant, however, the *tenor* line is not otherwise texted (which is the case for the majority of motets).

Above the line of borrowed music that forms the *tenor*, two lines have been added: the *motetus* (B in Figure 1) and the *triplum* (C in Figure 1). The *tenor* is not texted save for the identification of 'In seculum' at the beginning.[13] The *motetus* and *triplum*, however, are texted with two secular love songs: one laments the suffering felt at the hands of an arrogant lover, while the other begs a dark-haired lady to have pity on her lover. This short piece offers multiple angles for interpretation. The two texts of the upper lines sound against each other, suggesting consonances and dissonances of meaning as well as musical harmony. The sacred *tenor* 'In seculum' ('for ever') is appropriate to the love lyrics, but understood in context of the full sacred plainchant, we could make many further leaps of interpretation. Our purpose, however, is not to speculate on these possible readings. Instead, we are looking at the complexity of defining the metadata to be used in describing and classifying the motet in a way that allows medievalists with different research questions to make use of the data, regardless of their particular focus.

WHY THE MOTET IS COMPLEX DATA

To the complexity of how a motet is generated, we can add a further set of intricacies that may affect how motets are categorised and potentially encoded. The following categories help to elucidate some of the problems encountered in applying inflexible classifications that are derived from specific perspectives, i.e. music, text, or manuscript-focused approaches.

1. The tenor line

While the *tenor* line of a motet is usually derived from a section of sacred plainchant, it can be occasionally taken from the music and text of vernacular songs. Even if we set aside this complication, however, the data associated with the chant itself is manifold. In the example, 'In seculum' is extracted from the chant 'Hec dies' to create the *tenor* line. Aside from the translation of the extract and possible interpretations, the quoted chant is pointing to a particular section of the liturgy, and a particular kind of service and piece of music within it. For instance, 'Hec dies' is part of the Mass service. Because it is sung at Easter Masses, it has associations with a particular point on the calendar. Further, the text of the second half of the plainchant is drawn from Psalm 118:1. Hence, there is great potential to link motet metadata to metadata about the liturgy, the Church calendar, and the Bible.

2. Gennrich's Numbers

In the 1950s, scholar Friedrich Gennrich created a comprehensive bibliography of French and Latin motets composed in the wave of motet composition known as 'ars antiqua' ('old art/style'), to which the motet with which we are concerned belongs. Gennrich's technique was to categorise the motets according to their *tenors*. He first identified all the sections of the Mass and Office (daily prayers set to music) from which motet *tenors* were taken and gave each of these sections numbers. 'In seculum' comes from the chant numbered M13. It is important to note that M13 refers to the whole piece, and that the 'Hec dies', 'Domino', 'Domino Quoniam', and 'In seculum' *tenors* are all taken from this plainchant. Hence, citing the Gennrich number links 'In seculum' motets not just with other 'In seculum' motets, but with all motets drawn from the M13 spectrum. Gennrich's method of organizing information creates further conundra. The *moteti*, *tripla*, and *quadrupla*, which form the upper lines of the motets, are numbered individually by Gennrich. This method takes into account that individual lines of motets occasionally appear elsewhere—in other motets, for example—or that a motet may be rewritten with a new *triplum*. However, Gennrich's numbers apply to the *textual* line only and not the associated musical line. In cases where that line of music appears with different text (a *contrafactum*), Gennrich gives that line a different number. This may be problematic for some musicologists; however, in order to produce a workable catalogue, Gennrich had to choose an organizing principle, and for him text was a more expedient choice.

3. Different versions in manuscripts

A number of motets occur in more than one manuscript. In some cases the text and music are identical between one manuscript and another, however, variations are frequent. This can mean a difference of just an odd word or musical note here and there, which is adequately explained with a critical note in an edition. However, it can also mean a more substantial variation, such as an alternative text for one or more of the musical lines, an additional line of music and text, fewer lines of music and text, or an edition of just text, etc. The possibilities for variation and adaptation are multiple. Our example motet, 'Trop sovent me dueil / Brunete a qui j'ai mon cuer done / In seculum', can elucidate this. The piece occurs in the Montpellier Codex (Montpellier, Faculté de Médecine MS H 196), a thirteenth-century source that contains 345 items, of which nearly all are motets. It is also found in the Bamberg Manuscript (Bamberg, Staatsbibliothek, Lit. 115 (olim Ed. IV. 6.)), another source largely devoted to motets. The texts only of the *triplum* and the *motetus* are found in a Vatican Library MS (Rome, Bibl. Vat. Reg., lat. 1490); the music of the *tenor* and *triplum* lines occurs with the *triplum* re-texted in Latin in a Munich manuscript (Munich, Bayer. Staatsbibl., lat. 5539), and later in that same manuscript the music of the *tenor* and *motetus* lines is found with the *motetus* re-texted in Latin. The textual *incipit* (opening textual line) of the *motetus* appears in the manuscript Besançon, Bibl.

mun. I, 716. Some motets are also quoted in music treatises. Thus, at a very basic level, the variability of differing versions may be summarised as follows:

a.   versions with one or more lines of different music
b.   versions with one or more lines of different text
c.   fewer total lines
d.   more total lines
e.   examples with just a text of a motet line
f.   a reference in a treatise on music

4. Links to other compositions

In addition to borrowing music for their *tenors*, motets may cite snippets of other genres of song or even non-musical genres in their upper lines. For example, in 'Trop sovent me dueil / Brunete a qui j'ai mon cuer done / In seculum', the final line of the *motetus* ('A ma dame ai mis mon cuer et mon pense') is found—text and music—in two other motets and three secular songs. Many of the texts of song extracts found in motets have been identified and catalogued by Nico H. J. van den Boogaard.[14] As such, there is the potential to identify these connections, too, by linking a citation from a given motet with other compositions, thus indicating the way a motet, or parts of it, connect with other musical and textual compositions.

5. Multiple naming conventions

What makes the motet particularly fitting for a case study is the complexity of its naming and identification. Our example motet 'Trop sovent me dueil / Brunete a qui j'ai mon cuer done / In seculum' can be referred to by multiple means:

a.   The full title 'Trop sovent me dueil / Brunete a qui j'ai mon cuer done / In seculum' is a clear way of indicating the piece of music in question. However, it is a cumbersome title and it does not refer to a manuscript source.
b.   Often within the context of articles and essays about motets, writers will shorten a title after the first reference. Our example motet may therefore become 'Trop / Brunete / In seculum'—a useful contraction, but potentially confusing to a search engine.
c.   In medieval treatises on music, and also in indices for MSS containing motets, the *incipit* of the *motetus* frequently denotes the motet (for our example: 'Brunete a qui j'ai mon cuer done').
d.   As outlined above, each *tenor* source and the individual upper textual lines have been catalogued and numbered by Gennrich. Our example motet has the identifiers 172 (Tr) and 173 (M) with *tenor* source number M 13 Grad.

e. Our motet is frequently known as Mo85 because it is the eighty-fifth item in the Montpellier Codex. Since this codex is by far the most extensive source for motets, 'Mo' numbering is a popular convention in scholarly articles. However, Mo85 is also the seventeenth item in the Bamberg MS and may therefore also be known as Ba17 (the MSS also take these common short versions of their names, Montpellier for instance being contracted to 'Mo').

An example of this complexity at work: in Hans Tischler's modern edition of the Montpellier Codex, the last line of the *motetus* 'Trop sovent me dueil / Brunete a qui j'ai mon cuer done / In seculum' has been marked as a citation.[15] To find out where else this citation appears, we can consult van den Boogaard's catalogue (in French), which indicates that two further motets contain this snippet of text. However, van den Boogaard gives only the Gennrich numbers of the lines in which the quotations appear. We must then turn to Gennrich's catalogue (in German). Gennrich gives the textual incipit of each numbered line, as well as the manuscript sources and folio numbers, and we discover that the other two motets are also in the Montpellier Codex. However, Tischler numbers the motets by their order in Montpellier and does not refer to the Gennrich numbers, and we must therefore refer to the alphabetical contents list in vol. I of Tischler in order to be directed to a motet in vol. II, and another in vol. III. The seasoned motet researcher does not generally balk at this journey through five books (which are rare and largely out of print) and three languages (not including the Middle French and Latin!), but it can make the repertory daunting for newcomers, be they academics, students, or interested amateurs.

Scholars have been reluctant to organise motet data too rigidly because of these intricacies and the manner in which motets evolve and change across sources. If we privilege text, like Gennrich, then this is at the expense of the music. If we privilege a version in one MS, this obscures the variations inherent to the motet genre, expressed through the different instantiations across MSS. What is required is a flexible format that emphasises the mutability and modularity of these musical curios, rather than trying to fit them to inappropriate and rigid categories.

TOWARDS ENCODING MOTET DATA

The ability of LOD to express as many links as is desirable, without having to agree on (despite having to clearly define) metadata, makes it a viable candidate to articulate the intersecting and overlapping data that not only make up but also extend from and to the motet microcosm. There are currently projects which are encoding motet texts and music. For example, the archive of medieval French lyrics 'Je chante ung chant' has a number of motet texts marked up in the

Text Encoding Initiative (TEI) P5-conformant XML, while the Music Encoding Initiative (MEI) is being explored as a means to encode both music and text in XML.[16] These XML systems organise data hierarchically, with the purpose of encoding complete pieces of text or music in a robust yet interoperable manner that enables detailed searching within the texts or musical pieces in a given archive, but not across archives. This offers good solutions for many medieval data problems. For example, the ability to encode variant readings from different source texts means a digital edition can incorporate multiple versions in a way a print edition cannot (the 'Je Chante' site is an excellent example of this). However, the hierarchical structure can imply connections or dependencies where there are none (the 'Je Chante' site encodes each text by choosing one MS as a 'primary' source and relating all the others to it, even though the other MSS may not be direct copies of it).

Using the Resource Description Framework (RDF), LOD may also employ XML (in which case it is referred to as RDF/XML), or other RDF serialization formats such as Turtle, N3 or JSON-LD, primarily to express connections between things on the web in serialized, machine-readable formats. However, LOD is non-hierarchical. RDF is focussed on metadata, and is based on making and encoding statements about things in a subject-predicate-object format (called a *triple*). The subjects are designated persistent identifiers, and the predicate is used to assign a value or property (the object) to the subject. Hence:

'motet x' (subject) **'has the language'** (predicate) **'French'** (object)

However, a subject can also be an object, so predicates can link persistent identifiers. Here 'motet x' becomes the object in the expression:

'manuscript x' (subject) **'contains'** (predicate) **'motet x'** (object)

What this means simply is that links between data can be created in a non-hierarchical fashion. Via RDF-based encoding, LOD will therefore allow the generation of semantic connections between the most granular motet metadata and larger generic concepts, and vice versa. That the data is designated as *open* means that URIs representing the subjects, objects, and predicates created will be accessible for use and being linked to by others working with motets, creating even greater possibilities for the establishment of the relationships between data points. Such an organisation of knowledge will allow researchers—medieval musicologists, but also researchers as a general category—to dive into the material democratically laid out, and approach it from multiple perspectives, be it text, manuscript, or music centered, and regardless of their training in the conventions of the field.

Our next step is to work towards a proof-of-concept prototype that will demonstrate how motet data can be encoded, and subsequently searched and employed in research. To create this we need to severely limit the amount of data to be initially encoded. To encode hundreds of motets and their associated data, and then express all the links between them is a truly mammoth task. In choosing a set of motets for a proof of concept that demonstrates the application of LOD to motets, we have limited ourselves to certain factors in order to restrict the complexity, and thus provide a clear example. We have chosen to focus on one *tenor* source only. 'In seculum' appeared to be a good choice because it was one of the most popular *tenor* lines of the thirteenth-century motet repertory and provided us with a good selection of motets—72 in fact. We have limited the selection further to three-part motets (those with a *tenor*, *motetus*, and *triplum*, but no *quadruplum*) whose upper lines are in French (hence any motets with Latin-texted upper lines were eliminated), and which appear in the Montpellier codex. This has left us with a reasonable selection of 16 motets. Since they share a number of common factors, this limits considerably the complexity of the data set, while still providing us with sufficient range to show how the motet data would benefit from the application of LOD encoding.

In addition to the limiting of our data set, we have omitted a good deal of other data and connections. In this iteration we are not including folio numbers of MS, links to MSS images, detailed information about the MSS, nor any references to modern editions or facsimiles. Instances of texts transmitted without music have been left out. We are leaving out information about identified citations since this would bring in references to other genres of music and literature. There will also be no bibliographic references. All these data, and potentially a vast deal more, will be crucial to add in future iterations.

The areas we have identified as key are the naming conventions, the identity of individual lines, the Gennrich numbers, the manuscripts in which the motets are found, the shelfmarks and common names of the manuscripts, the numbering given to the motets in both the Montpellier and Bamberg MSS, and the language of the texts (which would of course be mainly French except for the 'In seculum' *tenor*). As such our subject categories are:

- The three-part name of each motet
- The individual names of each line
- Gennrich identification numbers for each part
- Gennrich *tenor* source identification numbers
- The manuscripts in which these motets appear/are mentioned
- Montpellier Codex numbers
- Bamberg Manuscript numbers
- Languages

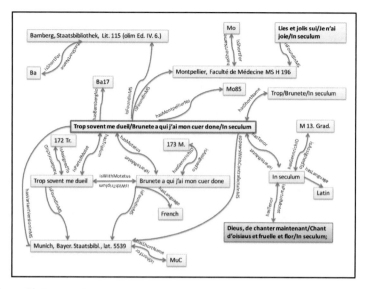

Figure 3. Subset of motet data relationships from our selected group of items.

Under these categories we have formulated lists of subjects (which will be given persistent identifiers), most of which are also used as objects. These are fully laid out in the Appendix. Using these subjects we have considered how they are connected to one another, and created a list that articulates all the interrelationships in our limited proof-of-concept data set. This has generated a preliminary set of predicates (also given in the Appendix). Even with our purposely limited data, we have a spreadsheet of interrelationships that is over 550 lines in length. To provide the reader with an idea of the connections, we have put a small subset of this data into diagrammatic form.

Figure 3 highlights some of the relationships associated with our example motet 'Trop sovent me dueil / Brunete a qui j'ai mon cuer done / In seculum'. Even within our already highly-limited subset, we have had to omit some connections for clarity. Nonetheless, the complexity of the naming and numbering conventions is apparent. Green is used here to show the constellation of information associated with the central motet. The items shown in blue and purple are there to demonstrate where other motets can relate to our example motet, in this case by sharing a *tenor*, or being in the same manuscript, although the interconnections could easily be far more complex.

NEXT STEPS

We have aimed to show the complexity of the metadata surrounding the thirteenth-century motet. LOD will be an ideal means for navigating this maze of information because it will allow for the data to be presented in a non-hierarchical fashion. For a genre that shows high variability across manuscripts and that has multiple lines of text *and* music (which themselves can operate independently) this is extremely important. Researchers and students are currently limited to negotiating multiple volumes, whose naming conventions do not synchronise. They are also confounded by certain metadata being privileged over others for the expediencies of publishing and cataloguing.

Figure 3 gives us a small glimpse of the possibilities. By encoding motet metadata according to LOD principles, the network of this data could be encountered and explored from any point, rather than through the particular point of view of one editor or cataloguer. With machine-readable metadata, statistical information on *tenors*, chant sources, languages, citations, etc. could be generated instantly, substantially reducing research time and paving the way for the discovery of hitherto unnoticed connections.

A proof-of-concept encoding of our data is the next step. However, in the longer term the task ahead is truly enormous. Aside from the issue of moving from a very small sample subset to a much larger and considerably more varied set of data, we must also coordinate with the community of researchers to fine-tune the ontology for motet studies—to understand what kinds of connections are being made between data points, what sort of questions are being asked, and how can the community be best served by this endeavour. Despite the size of the task it is well worth the effort because of LOD's non-hierarchical and flexible potential in organizing and linking complex data.

APPENDIX: SUBJECTS/OBJECTS AND PREDICATES

The three-part name of each motet*
NB: We have not supplied the short version of each name, since it will usually be the first word or two of the triplum and motetus and the full tenor.

Trop sovent me dueil / Brunete a qui j'ai mon cuer done / In seculum;
Dieus, de chanter maintenant / Chant d'oisiaus et fuelle et flor / In seculum;
Lies et jolis sui / Je n'ai joie / In seculum;
He, tres douces amouretes / D'amors esloignies / In seculum;
L'autrier trouvai une plesant tousete / L'autrier, les une espinete / In seculum;
En son service amourous / Tant est plesaint, bien faite / In seculum;
Trop fu li regart amer / J'ai si mal, n'i puis durer / In seculum;
A une ajornee s'est Margot / Doce dame, en qui dangier / In seculum;
On doit fine amor / La biaute ma dame / In seculum;
Ja n'amerai autre que / Sire Dieus, li doz maus m'ocit / In seculum;
J'ai les biens d'amours / Que ferai, biau sire Dieus? Li regart / In seculum;
Se gries m'est au cuers / A qui dirai les maus / In seculum;

Bons amis, je vos rendrai / Qu'ai je forfait ne mespris / In seculum;
En non Diu, que que nus die, trop a celi / En non Diu, que que nus die,
l'amor / In seculum;
Quant se depart li jolis tans / He, cuer joli! Trop m'aves / In seculum;
Puisqu'en amer loiaument me sui mis / Quant li jolis tans doit entrer / In
seculum;

The individual names of each line
Tripla
Trop sovent me dueil; Dieus, de chanter maintenant; Lies et jolis sui; He,
tres douces amouretes; L'autrier trouvai une plesant tousete; En son service
amourous; Trop fu li regart amer; A une ajornee s'est Margot; On doit fine
amor; Ja n'amerai autre que; J'ai les biens d'amours; Se gries m'est au cuers;
Bons amis, je vos rendrai; En non Diu, que que nus die, trop a celi; Quant se
depart li jolis tans; Puisqu'en amer loiaument me sui mis

Moteti
Brunete a qui j'ai mon cuer done; Chant d'oisiaus et fuelle et flor; Je n'ai
joie; D'amors esloignies; L'autrier, les une espinete; Tant est plesaint, bien
faite; J'ai si mal, n'i puis durer; Doce dame, en qui dangier; La biaute ma
dame; Sire Dieus, li doz maus m'ocit; Que ferai, biau sire Dieus? Li regart;
A qui dirai les maus; Qu'ai je forfait ne mespris; En non Diu, que que nus
die, l'amor; He, cuer joli! Trop m'aves; Quant li jolis tans doit entrer

Tenors
In seculum

Gennrich identification numbers for each part
172; 173; 176; 177; 178; 179; 180; 181; 182; 183; 184; 185; 158; 157; 154;
155; 187; 186; 211; 212; 188; 189; 190; 191; 193; 192; 194; 195

Gennrich Tenor Source Identification Numbers
M 13. Grad.

The manuscripts in which these motets appear/are mentioned
Full shelfmarks
Arras fragment (lost)
Bamberg, Staatsbibliothek, Lit. 115 (olim Ed. IV. 6.);
Madrid, Bibl. Nac., 20486;
Metz, Bibl. mun., 535 (lost);
Montpellier, Faculté de Médecine MS H 196;
Munich, Bayer. Staatsbibl., lat. 5539;

Paris, Bibl. Nat., fr. 12786;
Paris, Bibl. Nat., mouv. acq. françaises 13521 (La Clayette MS);
Rome, Bibl. Vat. Reg., lat. 1490;
Wolfenbüttel, Herzog-August-Bibl., 1206 (*olim* Helmstad. 1099);

Short names the manuscripts are known by
12786; Ba; Bes; Cl; Ma; Metz; Mo; MuC; V; W2;

Montpellier Codex Numbers
Mo85; Mo87; Mo102; Mo107; Mo118; Mo120; Mo132; Mo133; Mo134;
Mo137; Mo138; Mo162; Mo163; Mo166; Mo324; Mo336

Bamberg Manuscript Numbers
Ba17; Ba104;

Languages
French; Latin

Predicates
hasTriplum; hasMotetus; hasTenor; hasGennrichID; isFoundInMS;
hasMontpellierNo; hasBambergNo; hasVariantVersionInMS; hasLanguage;
isPartofMotet; isWithMotetus; isWithTenor; appearsWithContrafactainMS;
appearsAsDifferentLineInMS; appearsWithoutTextInMS; isAssignedTo;
hasShortName; isShortFor

END NOTES

[1] The authors wish to thank Alexandra Bolintineanu, Matthew Evan Davis, Carl Stahmer, and Bridget Whearty for their comments on earlier drafts of this article.

[2] E. Turnator, et. al, 'Summary of proceedings for the 'Linking the Middle Ages' workshop' (May 11–12, 2015) is available in full at this link: http://dx.doi.org/10.15781/T2MW2C. Last accessed 1 August 2015.

[3] See http://5stardata.info/, last accessed 1 August 2015; http://linkeddata.org/, last accessed 1 August 2015. Also see, E. Turnator, et. al. 'Summary of proceedings', 51–56.

[4] A URI is a string of characters that identifies an abstract or physical resource. For the distinction between URIs and URLs see: https://en.wikipedia.org/wiki/Uniform_resource_identifier#The_relationship_between_URIs.2C_URLs.2C_and_URNs, last accessed 1 August 2015. Also see, https://tools.ietf.org/html/rfc3986#section-1.1.2, last accessed 7 November 2015.

[5] Leif Isaksen's observations in E. Turnator, 'Summary of proceedings', 56.

[6] E. Turnator, et. al. 'Summary of proceedings,' 52.

[7] For a fuller description of the Christian Mass and the place of liturgical chant within it see James W. McKinnon, et al., 'Mass', *Grove Music Online, Oxford Music Online*, (Oxford, 2000): http://www.oxfordmusiconline.com/subscriber/article/grove/music/45872, last accessed 1 August 2015.

[8] For the history and styles of Plainchant see Kenneth Levy, et al., 'Plainchant', *Grove Music Online, Oxford Music Online*, (Oxford, 2000): http://www.oxfordmusiconline.com/subscriber/article/grove/music/40099, last accessed 1 August 2015.

[9] See section I of Ernest H. Sanders, et al., 'Motet', *Grove Music Online, Oxford Music Online*, (Oxford, 2000): http://www.oxfordmusiconline.com/subscriber/article/grove/music/40086pg1, last accessed 1 August 2015. For a detailed account of the development of the motet see Mark Everist, *French Motets in the Thirteenth Century: Music, Poetry and Genre*, (Cambridge, 1994), chapters 1–3.

[10] Christopher Page, 'Johannes de Grocheio on secular music: a corrected text and a new translation', *Plainsong and Medieval Music*, 2 (1993).

[11] Page, 'Johannes de Grocheio', 36.

[12] *Translation from 'Haec dies', ChoralWiki*: http://www1.cpdl.org/wiki/index.php/Haec_dies, last accessed 1 August 2015.

[13] This has led to some debate over whether a *tenor* line would be sung or played on an instrument, and if the former, then whether to the given chant words or to a vowel sound.

[14] Nico H. J. van den Boogaard, *Rondeaux et refrains du XXIIe siècle au début du XIVe.* (Paris, 1969).

[15] Tischler, Hans, ed., *The Montpellier Codex*, 4 vols, (Madison, 1978).

[16] See, http://jechante.exeter.ac.uk/archive/, last accessed 1 August 2015. The Text Encoding Initiative (TEI) 'is a consortium which collectively develops and maintains a standard for the representation of texts in digital form.' (See http://www.tei-c.org/index.xml). P5 is the current version of the TEI guidelines. MEI website: http://music-encoding.org/, last accessed 1 August 2015.

MODELING THE HUMANITIES: DATA LESSONS FROM THE WORLD OF EDUCATION

ARMANDA LEWIS

Abstract   *This article will explore advances in the field of educational data modeling that have implications for modeling humanistic data. Traditional humanistic inquiry, bolstered by micro-analyses conducted by the scholar, has made way for machine-assisted methods that parse and quantify large amounts of qualitative data to reveal possible trends and focus more analogue approaches. At best, this play between human- and machine-directed approaches can lead to more profound explorations of texts. In this exploration of qualitative-quantitative methodologies that leverage human agency and machine-directed techniques, I suggest a mixed methods approach for dealing with the humanities. Specifically, this discussion will analyze the current methodological tensions related to Educational Data Mining and Learning Analytics to reveal best practices for modeling humanistic data.*

Principle questions of interest in this essay include: What defines literary "big data? How can we define DH modeling and where does it depart from traditional data modeling? What role does machine-based modeling have in the context of the scholarly close read? What can we learn from educational data modeling practices that are in the midst of resolving tensions between human-machine patterning?

Keywords: educational data modeling, learning analytics, computational analysis, 'big' data, human-machine patterning

International Journal of Humanities and Arts Computing 10.1 (2016): 51–62
DOI: 10.3366/ijhac.2016.0159
© Edinburgh University Press 2016
www.euppublishing.com/journal/ijhac

While literary digital humanities (DH) scholarship has made advances in the areas of descriptive analyzing, parsing and visualizing, an emerging area remains DH modeling.[1] Modeling, the creation of a generalizable representation of a concept or phenomenon, exposes assumptions made about the underlying data. A statistical model, for example, works on two levels: it makes claims about a population based on aspects of a sub-group, and it uses finite quantitative data to describe or predict some construct.[2] Modeling the humanities is challenging given the mixed nature of humanistic big data, varying notions of what constitutes 'big' datasets, as well as evolving discussions on the role of the scholar in automated methods.[3] Not surprisingly humanist scholars have proposed an inclusive approach—text, artifact, and processable information—to qualifying humanities content, in part to account for the rich, messy, and constructed nature of the information, as well as the multiple possibilities for its manipulation and interpretation.[4] This interpretivist way of viewing data privileges multiple meanings and thick descriptions, differing from quantitative fields that make sense of data through synthesis and reductive means.[5]

One field that can inform humanities big data and modeling is that of education, with two of the main large data perspectives being Educational Data Mining and Learning Analytics and Knowledge. Educational data, like humanities data, is disjointed, multimodal, and recognized for its interpretability.[6] Frameworks and perspectives with which researchers engage with the information characterize results. It is the aim of this paper to highlight ways in which the current debates in modeling educational data can enrich and disrupt existing ways of examining the humanistic data model.

This article will explore advances in the field of educational data modeling that have implications for modeling humanistic data. Traditional humanistic inquiry, bolstered by micro-analyses conducted by the scholar, has made way for machine-assisted methods that parse and quantify large amounts of qualitative data to reveal possible trends and focus more analogue approaches. At best, this play between human- and machine-directed approaches can lead to more profound explorations of texts. In this exploration of qualitative-quantitative methodologies that leverage human agency and machine-directed techniques, I suggest a mixed-methods approach for dealing with the humanities: What defines literary big data? How can we define DH modeling and where does it depart from traditional data modeling? What role does machine-based modeling have in the context of the scholarly close read? What can we learn from educational data modeling practices that are in the midst of resolving tensions between human-machine patterning? Mixed methods, a methodological approach within the social sciences, has potential for DH since it reconciles diverse approaches, and challenges the scholar to be explicit about adopting methods that stem from opposing epistemological roots. DH is still at a stage of heavy experimentation, still waiting for DH-born methodologies that reflect new types of knowledge. Educational Data Mining and Learning Analytics and Knowledge are two fields within education with potential for DH since they consolidate various and large streams of information, while privileging the role of the researcher in interpreting findings.

WHAT IS A (HUMANITIES) MODEL?

Big Data, a movement spanning disciplines, implies the harnessing of computational power to parse large amounts of ultimately quantifiable information for distillation and subsequent steps in the mining process.[7] Heralded as a knowledge necessity, the understanding of big data potentially can reveal patterns, offer personalized interactions, and address the integrity of stored information.[8] Humanities scholars, in keeping with an interpretivist lens, look beyond size when they write of big data in DH.[9] Notions such as raw data and data cleaning expose the constructed and perspectival nature of all information, as well as of the tools and methods used to parse and analyze such information.[10] In their discussion of humanities big data, scholars note the qualities of (1) largeness in size, (2) multiplicity of meaning, (3) diversity of form, and (4) level of interconnectedness focusing on the richness, rather than the sheer quantity of information.[11] For humanities scholars, big data maintains the complexity of smaller data—but magnifies it exponentially.

Just as data has multiple meanings, so does the notion of the model.[12] The current conception of model refers to a computable abstraction that is general enough to define specific instances of a concept. Literary models focus on cultural- or language-based abstractions that go beyond the contexts of original creation while being deeply positioned within these contexts.[13] The literary corpus, large collections of linked texts, and the way in which machine-based methods can detect patterns and reveal abstractions within such collections are one such example. Big cultural data—vis a via Frédéric Kaplan's map for DH big data research, in which the two stages of pattern recognition and simulation and inference–are the most directly related to modeling.[14] Two types of humanities big data models exist from this work and are reflected in educational big data. One is that a model can be constructed and used to detect characteristics automatically, useful for classification and descriptive purposes. The second is a model that can, with the information entered, predict new patterns and simulate nonexistent data.

THE NATURE OF EDUCATIONAL DATA AND MODELING

Education scholars seek to understand various facets of the educational process, including assessment, curricula creation, the design of online and physical environments, and the political, psychological, and socio-cultural underpinnings of informal and formal learning and teaching. Sources of inquiry include statistical and survey data, interview transcripts, video and platform logs, learner-produced artifacts (e.g. compositions, designs, concept maps), and more. With the rise of digital tools and environments increasingly mediated by such tools, researchers find themselves with access to more data per student, as well as more types of data. Digital games for learning, for example, can be delivered to hundreds of thousands of participants, with the capability of recording users' individual actions online and adapting to those actions. Researchers supplement this log data with behavioral observations, sensor data, rich interviews, surveys, and video recordings, along with non-gameplay information such as test scores and demographic data.[15] Similar educational environments include intelligent tutoring systems, open-ended learning environments, and simulations, and as evidenced by these examples, we will focus on learning-related data.

Given the multimodal and sizeable nature of this new genre of educational data, researchers have responded in several ways. They employ quantitative and qualitative social science methods to parse and make sense of complex information. Increasingly, these mixed methods, which acknowledge the benefit of incorporating statistical and human-led analyses, are leveraged to enrich the exploration at hand.[16] The recognized validity of mixed methods reflects (1) an epistemological shift that recognizes multiple ways in which a researcher can claim knowledge (e.g., positivist, constructivist, or interpretivist), as well as (2) a paradigm for leveraging two historically opposing research perspectives. There are several flavors of mixed methods research, including the sequential use of one method to confirm or expand on results achieved from another method, or the concurrent use of methods to enrich the overall analysis.[17] Still, there are others who adopt a mixed methods approach to modeling. Quantitative tools have the ability to predict and summarize, while qualitative tools have the ability to describe richly and highlight the range of the data. In modeling practice, researchers use quantitative methods to summarize and quickly parse through large datasets, the results of which will feed into models that categorize and predict future behavior. They then incorporate the targeted use of qualitative methods to inform future actions and provide rich, contextual understandings of numerical data. There are many scholars who argue that mixed methods, particularly those that leverage participatory methods and maintain a healthy tension between reductionist and interpretivist perspectives, make research more diverse and emancipatory by recognizing different types of evidence.[18]

DEALING WITH EDUCATIONAL DATA: TWO APPROACHES AND THEIR
RELEVANCE TO THE HUMANITIES

This section examines how the field of education manages large multimodal data, what constitutes two major approaches—Educational Data Mining and Learning

Analytics and Knowledge—, and which aspects have the most potential for humanistic data and DH analytic methods.[19]

Educational Data Mining (EDM) and Learning Analytics and Knowledge (LAK) have emerged as two of three primary schools to analyze the copious data that come from learners' performance-based processes, interactions and the environments in which these take place.[20] Though both EDM and LAK measure knowledge dynamically over time, harness theory to inform analysis, and mine data to understand cognitive processes and inform decisions by various stakeholders, there are marked distinctions that relate to the role that machine-based data analysis plays in DH.

Educational Data Mining

EDM 'is concerned with developing, researching, and applying computerized methods to detect patterns in large collections of educational data' (Scheuer & McLaren, 2011), which is evidenced by a focus on the how, meaning understanding how processes make large datasets intelligible and how theories can underpin such processes (1075).[21] This knowledge can then be used to develop theory and additional methods and tools. Key to both the processes and the theories is the notion of automation; as such, we observe interpretivist / reductionist rhetoric that coincides with developing for machine consumption.

It is logical that since so much emphasis is placed on training and leveraging machine-based knowledge, EDM researchers would need to reduce learning to a series of discrete components, 'analyzing individual components and relationships between them' (253).[22] In major EDM reviews, acceptable methods all highlight machine learning techniques and algorithms (e.g., Bayesian Knowledge Tracing to map real-time learning, clustering to see groupings quickly), and human judgment is often subordinate to the ultimate goal of having the machine glean patterns, make recommendations, and personalize content and pathways.[23] This privileging of the machine-based model is logical, given the need for intelligent systems to parse large numbers of learners' actions, model learning or other variables in real time, and adapt accordingly. Many algorithms allow for machines to quickly parse data and detect behaviors based on that data. A canonical example is the Baker et al., study on gaming the system, in which a model is created to detect if large numbers of students engaging with a tutoring system are guessing, answering correctly, or gaming the system in order to increase points[24] The automated method was tested against human coders and received comparable categorization results. The main EDM lesson to apply to DH modeling is the role of the researcher in the creation of a machine-usable model. In the Baker example, researchers engaged in a technique called feature engineering, in which they carefully examined all possible variables that could be put into the model, and only selected those that were most relevant, with relevance determined by statistical techniques, importance to theory, as well as the researchers' best judgment. These variables are then given to the machine that then produces a data-mined model. Another technique, knowledge discovery, goes one step further and tasks the researcher with gaining expertise in theory and conceptual knowledge, and then creating the model.[25] Drucker has more recently called for a deeper understanding of the inner workings of an adopted tool or method.[26] I would argue that knowledge discovery has the greatest potential for DH since it places the creation of the model on the researcher, and privileges theory and decision justification that should be made explicit. A criticism of DH can be that there is not enough critique into the use of tools and algorithms, though growing cases of scholar-led design of systems are overturning this claim.[27] Sinclair, Ruecker, and Radzikowska describe *Mandala*, a browser 'which allows researchers to open a document or multiple documents at the same time and iteratively construct visual Boolean queries that draw on the underlying data (such as the XML-encoded version of *Romeo and Juliet* platform).[28] The resulting models generated by the non-automated mechanisms require the researcher to have an underlying thesis, which then forms the basis for the model that would then be entered into the browser. Results of the query are constructed in a way that parallels the knowledge discovery process for the educational data miner.

Learning Analytics and Knowledge

Ferguson (2012) associates learning analytics with 'optimis[ing] opportunities for online learning' and locates it at 'the level of courses and departments' (310), while Siemens (2013) stresses 'sensemaking and action' (1382).[29] LAK tends to be more practice-based and focused on the what and why, meaning understanding what data says about learning and why. This knowledge can then be used to improve learning situations. Because of this focus on the why, we observe numerous examples of LAK being used as a means to enhance the understanding of learning processes and environments, including those that rely on metadata, early warning, and recommendations.[30] These and other techniques imply an intermediary role that machine-based data-analysis plays. In contrast to EDM, which holds machine analysis as the main phase of the analytics process, LAK privileges human observation and interpretation. Siemens and Baker (2012) support this distinction, and add that LAK takes on a more holistic view of issues.[31] This corresponds to the place for human analysis, which works best getting the whole picture on something and understanding context and seeking rich descriptions.

If EDM has implications for how the DH researcher constructs a model and interfaces with a data mining tool, then LAK has much to in the way that feedback mechanisms function in DH modeling tools. One study examines the importance of distilling information to make complex computations intelligible for learned, but non-data mining audiences. DH tools could benefit from making underlying algorithms and the accompanying assumptions transparent.

HUMAN-LED, MACHINE-LED: A TALE OF TWO DH CITIES

The previous discussion relates to datasets within the humanities in three major ways. One is the need for both human-led and machine-led parsing of information, which has existed for decades. As the existence of digital information has increased, emerging considerations are the role that machine-led processes play in analyzing and modeling humanistic data. If we turn to larger datasets in particular, there becomes evident the need to reconcile these two ways of processing information. Another is the emergence of entitative versus interpretivist view of humanist big data. Often, the tools that DH scholars utilize to analyze and model data have been built from a reductionist perspective, so it is imperative that there is more attention paid to reconciling the oft-interpretivist view with which scholars analyze the outputs of such systems and the entitative view that the systems model and mine data. Allowing multiple types of evidence coincides with what Perloff calls differentials, or the interplay between the close read and Moretti's distant read, as well as between different perspectives.[32] Voyant allows for both single text mining as well as large cross corpora analyses, while topic modeling technologies that leverage Latent Dirichelet algorithms expose the caveats with which DH scholars must contend for the sake of mined topics.

The case of mixed methods within education data accords with that of literary DH, given the historical primacy of the close read and other human-led processes that match the creation of the artifact itself, with the growing presence of machine-produced parsing required for large corpora. Clement describes several projects in which she leverages the power of machine-led automation to reveal patterns, count words, and infer relationships. She then takes these outputs, aware of the underlying assumptions made by such platforms, and then gets to the business of interpretation, in all of its ambiguous glory.[33] Drucker remarks:

> I would argue that even for realist models, those that presume an observer-independent reality available to description, the methods of presenting ambiguity and uncertainty in more nuanced terms would be useful ... In statistical graphics the coordinate lines are always continuous and straight. In humanistic, interpretative, graphics, they might have breaks,

repetitions, and curves or dips. Interpretation is stochastic and probabilistic, not mechanistic, and its uncertainties require the same mathematical and computational models as other complex systems. Any humanistic study based on statistical methods, even the simplest techniques of counting, has to address the assumption involved in the categories on which such techniques ('how many of X') are based.[34]

This quote showcases the aim of the humanities to problematize and complicate, even in the face of tools and techniques that do the opposite. Using temporality as an example, she goes on to show that, while the social sciences and sciences have a linear understanding of clear cut 'variables', the humanities maintain the messiness inherent in information, and in our understanding of that information. Any model that is created must address that messiness, even if some smoothing is necessary, mandated by the tools available. Educational data scholars have managed to navigate the messiness and complexity of the original dataset, with the use of algorithms that, by definition strip the messiness and complexity to some degree.

Within literary studies, a suggested mixed methods approach entails utilizing quantitative approaches to summarize patterns and capture outlier information, while providing thick, layered interpretations. One essential aspect of adopting a mixed methods approach—quantitative and qualitative stages that collectively represent a reading—within literary studies, is to be explicit about the methods adopted. While this need not take the form of a literal methodology section within literary studies, I would argue for the articulation of how the quantitative and qualitative methods enhance one another and work to create the interpretation. Methodological stances within literary studies are usually hidden, since part of the reader's task is the active reconstruction of the author's methods and interpretation of the reasons for adopting such approaches. Part of this article's purpose is to highlight the epistemological conflicts at work between quantitative (traditionally reductionist) and qualitative (traditionally interpretivist) methods; therefore the recognition of methodological pluralism and how epistemological differences are negotiated within a study are needed to validate asserted claims. Mixed methods, an explicit methodology, as well as techniques that keep the researcher at the center of the model creation and interpretation process, are some techniques that DH scholars can leverage until native DH methods and methodologies are established. Because EDM and LAK have had success reconciling the interpretivist-reductionist tensions of large amounts of quantitative and qualitative data, address the essential roles that both machine analysis and human interpretation play in the research process, and have developed methods to position the scholar as uniquely capable of making sense of the outputs and generating abstractions, DH scholars should look to these emerging fields for inspiration.

END NOTES

[1] D. Hoover. 'Quantitative Analysis and Literary Studies', in S. Schreibman and R. Siemens eds., *A Companion to Digital Literary Studies* (Oxford: Blackwell, 2007), 517–33; J.-F. de Pasquale and J.-G. Meunier. 'Categorisation Techniques in Computer-Assisted Reading and Analysis of Texts (CARAT) in the Humanities', *Computers and the Humanities* 37:1 (2003), 111–18. K. Fitzpatrick, 'The humanities, done digitally, debates in the digital humanities', in M. Gold, ed., *Debates in the Digital Humanities*, (Minneapolis, MN: University of Minnesota Press, 2012), 12–15.

[2] W.D. Kelton and A.M. Law, *Simulation modeling and analysis* (Boston, 2000).; M.A. Serrano, A. Flammini and F. Menczer, 'Modeling statistical properties of written text', *PloS one*, 4.4, (2009), e5372.; L. Breiman, 'Statistical modeling: The two cultures (with comments and a rejoinder by the author)', *Statistical Science* 16.3 (2001), 199–231.

[3] This article uses the term humanities big data to refer to data that is large enough to warrant computational parsing. The humanities data that concerns this article technically could be categorized as medium data, meaning sizable enough to warrant machine assistance bit not large enough to compete with the complex computational processing speed and power necessary for analyzing neural and Google data. This latter data forms part of the Big Data movement, explained later in the article. For the purpose of this article, big and large humanities data is synonymous. We will concentrate on approaches to analyzing and modeling larger educational datasets (emphasis on learning) as they relate to large humanities data—Educational Data Mining and Learning Analytics and Knowledge.

[4] W. Pietz, 'Three Questions and One Experiment On Data Modeling in the Humanities', Workshop on Knowledge Organization and Data Modeling in the Humanities, (Brown University, Providence, RI), http://www.wwp.northeastern.edu/outreach/conference/kodm2012/piez/piez.pdf; C. Schöch, 'Big? Smart? Clean? Messy? Data in the Humanities'. *Journal of Digital Humanities* 2.3, (2013), http://journalofdigitalhumanities.org/2–3/big-smart-clean-messy-data-in-the-humanities/; S. Ramsay, *Reading Machines: Toward an Algorithmic Criticism* (Champaign: University of Illinois Press, 2011).; T. Owens, 'Defining Data for Humanists: Text, Artifact, Information or Evidence?', *Journal of Digital Humanities* 1.1 (2011), http://journalofdigitalhumanities.org/1–1/defining-data-for-humanists-by-trevor-owens/.

[5] C. Geertz, *The Interpretation of Cultures*, (New York, 1973).; J.S. Ward, and A. Barker, 'Undefined By Data: A Survey of Big Data Definitions', *ArXiv e-print*, (September 20, 2013), http://arxiv.org/abs/1309.5821.

[6] The concept of intelligence, for example, may refer to cognitive, emotional, or other types, and might be represented by the results of standardized tests, self-report surveys, and observational data, including coded observations and video. See B. Johnson and L. Christensen, *Educational research: Quantitative, qualitative, and mixed approaches* (New York, 2008). See also J.D. Mayer, D.R. Caruso and P. Salovey, 'Emotional intelligence meets traditional standards for an intelligence', *Intelligence*, 27, 4 (1999), 267–298.

[7] Diebold, Francis X. 2012. "A Personal Perspective on the Origin(s) and Development of 'Big Data': The Phenomenon, the Term, and the Discipline, Second Version." PIER Working Paper No. 13–003, November 26, 2012. http://ssrn.com/abstract=2202843; http://dx.doi.org/10.2139/ssrn.2202843.

[8] J. Manyika, M. Chui, B. Brown, J. Bughin, R. Dobbs, C. Roxburgh, A. Hung Byers, 'Big data: the next frontier for innovation, competition, and productivity' (2011), McKinsey & Company. http://www.mckinsey.com/insights/business_technology/big_data_the_next_frontier_for_innovation.

[9] Interpretivist points of view embrace emergent, thick, socially-constructed approaches that oppose positivist approaches that privilege reductionist, convergent explanations,

10 For works that present all data as constructed, see, L. Gitelman, *Raw Data" Is an Oxymoron* (Cambridge, MA: MIT Press, 2013).; M.L. Jockers, *Macroanalysis: Digital Methods and Literary History* (Urbana: Univ. of Illinois Press, 2013).; W. Kent, *Data and Reality*, 2nd ed, (Bloomington, IN: 1st Books, 2000).

11 d. boyd and K. Crawford, 'Six provocations for Big Data,' Social Science Research Network, (Rochester, NY, SSRN Scholarly Paper ID 1926431, Sep. 2011).; A. S. Levi. 'Humanities 'Big Data', *IEEE International Conference on Big Data* (2013), https://bighumanities.files.wordpress.com/2013/09/2_5_levi_paper.pdf; N. Bruügger and N. O. Finnemann, 'The Web and digital humanities: Theoretical and methodological concerns,' *Journal of Broadcasting & Electronic Media*, 57 (2013), 66–80.; C. L. Borgman, *Scholarship in the digital age: Information, infrastructure, and the Internet.* (Cambridge, MA: The MIT Press, 2010).

12 D.M. Bailer-Jones, *Models, Metaphors and Analogies*, in P. Machamer and M. Silberstein, eds., *Philosophy of Science*, (Oxford: Blackwell, 2002), 108–27.; R. Davis, H. Shrobe, and P. Szolovits, 'What Is Knowledge Representation?', *AI Magazine* (1993), 17–33., http://www.aaai.org/Library/Magazine/Voll4/l4 01.html, M.I. Finley, *Ancient History: Evidence and Models*, (New York: Viking, 1986).; N. Frye, *Literary and Mechanical Models*, in ed. I. Lancashire, ed., *Research in Humanities Computing 1. Papers from the 1989 ACH-ALLC Conference*, (Oxford: Clarendon Press, 1991), 1–12.; E.A. Lloyd, *Models*, in *Routledge Encyclopedia of Philosophy*, (London: Routledge, 1998).

13 W. McCarty, 'Modeling: A Study in Words and Meaning', in S. Schreibman, R. Siemens, J. Unsworth, eds., *A Companion to Digital Humanities*, (Oxford: Blackwell, 1994).; F. Moretti, *Graphs, Maps, Trees: Abstract Models for a Literary History*, (London: Verso, 2005).

14 F. Kaplan, 'A map for big data research in digital humanities', *Frontiers in Digital Humanities*, 2,1 (2015), 1–7. DOI = 10.3389/fdigh.2015.00001. http://journal.frontiersin.org/article/10.3389/fdigh.2015.00001/full.

15 B.D. Homer, J.L. Plass, & L. Blake, 'The effects of video on cognitive load and social presence in computer-based multimedia-learning', *Computers in Human Behavior*, 24(2008), 786–797.

16 Mixed methods has been a widely accepted research approach since the mid 1990s. J.W. Creswell, *Research design: Qualitative, quantitative, and mixed methods approaches*, 2nd ed. (SaThousand Oaks, California: Sage, 2003).; J.W. Creswell and V.L. Plano Clark, *Designing and conducting mixed methods research.* (2nd ed., (Thousand Oaks, CA: Sage, 2011).

17 J.C. Greene, *Mixed methods in social inquiry,* (San Francisco: John Wiley & Sons, 2007).; R.B. Johnson, A.J. Onwuegbuzie, and L.A. Turner, 'Toward a definition of mixed methods research'. *Journal of Mixed Methods Research*, 1(2007), 112–133.; D.L. Morgan, 'Paradigms lost and pragmatism regained: Methodological implications of combining qualitative and quantitative methods', *Journal of Mixed Methods Research*, 1(12007, 48–76.

18 D. Selener, *Participatory action research and social change*, (Cornell, NY: The Cornell Participatory Action Research Network, Cornell University, 1997).; D.M. Mertens, *Research and evaluation in education and psychology: Integrating diversity with quantitative, qualitative, and mixed methods.* (Thousand Oaks, CA: Sage Publications, 2014).

19 A third large educational data perspective is "Big Data". In contrast to EDM and LAK, which use theory and informed models to varying degrees to make analysis decisions, the Big Data perspective posits, rhetorically if not in practice, that large enough datasets can yield meaningful patterns to drive decision making, with or without theoretical grounding. Supporters are confident in the "follow the data" idea and argue that big data can model complex, messy phenomena, like human learning and behavior. See A.Y. Halevy, P. Norvig, F. Pereira, 'The unreasonable effectiveness of data', *IEEE Intelligent Systems*, 24 (2009), 8–12. Similar to EDM but in contrast to LAK, big data puts much faith in machine learning. Eric Ottem's blog (http://bigdataperspectives.com/) notes that "With machines we provide a structured environment first, and then hope they can learn the subtleties of a complex

world", which raises a fundamental contrast to the unstructured way that people first learn and then prepares them to continue learning in complicated environments. LAK recognizes that machine automation lacks the ability to completely explain processes as complex as human learning, while Big Data subordinates human interpretation, even more than does EDM. EDM leaves an important space for human input, if not at the analysis stage, then certainly at the initial conceptual stage. Theoretical grounding, human-based framing of an issue, is as important for EDM as it is for LAK. Even feature engineering, which discovers through iterative manipulation of the data, is based on some theoretical perspective. The big data method can be problematic when applied to learning. Whereas EDM and LAK use cross validation to make sure that claims made for one dataset's population is contextualized for different populations, the big data perspective can fall into the danger of gleaning short-term patterns without any attempt to contextualize them more broadly for time lapses and different groups.

[20] For context, EDM originates from data mining, and has pulled from psychometrics and intelligent tutor research to emerge as a distinct field. Education is messy, and EDM has responded by its own appropriate goodness of fit measures and a method in the spirit of "grounded theory" (ex. discovery through models). Though some call LAK a fully formed field, the nascent LAK is more of a research community given its shared vision of a problem but lack of agreed-upon canonical methods and fuzzy disciplinary borders. LAK also pulls from data mining, in addition to social network analysis and cognitive modeling techniques. LAK departs from academic analytic roots that are historically institutional and drills down to inform teachers and students directly.

[21] O. Scheuer, and B.M. Mclaren, Educational Data Mining, in N. Seel, ed., *Encyclopedia of the Sciences of Learning* (New York: Springer, 2011).

[22] G. Siemens and R.S.J.d. Baker, Learning Analytics and Educational Data Mining: Towards Communication and Collaboration (2009). *Proceedings of the 2nd International Conference on Learning Analytics and Knowledge.*

[23] R.S.J.d. Baker and K. Yacef, 'The State of Educational Data Mining in 2009: A Review and Future Visions', *Journal of Educational Data Mining*, 1,1 (2009), 3–17.

[24] R.S.J.d. Baker, A.T. Corbett, I. Roll, and K.R. Koedinger, 'Developing a Generalizable Detector of When Students Game the System', *User Modeling and User-Adapted Interaction*, 18, 3 (2008), 287–314.

[25] I. Roll, V. Aleven, B. M. McLaren, and K. R. Koedinger, 'Improving students' help-seeking skills using metacognitive feedback in an intelligent tutoring system', *Learning and Instruction* 21 (2011), http://www.cs.cmu.edu/~bmclaren/pubs/RollEtAl-ImprovingHelpSeekingWithITS-LandI2011.pdf.

[26] J. Drucker, 'Humanistic Theory and Digital Scholarship', in M. Gold, ed, *Debates in the Digital Humanities* (Minneapolis, 2012), 85–95.

[27] S. Sinclair, Ruecker, S. Gabriele, and A. Sapp, 'Digital Scripts on a Virtual Stage: The Design of New Online Tools for Drama Students,' *Proceedings of the Fifth IASTED International Conference on Web-Based Education* (Anaheim: ACTA, 2006), 155–59.; L. Burnard and S. Bauman, eds. *TEI P5: Guidelines for Electronic Text Encoding and Interchange*. Version 2.5.0. (Charlottesville, VA: Text Encoding Initiative Consortium, 2003). http://www.tei-c.org/Vault/P5/2.5.0/doc/tei-p5-doc/en/html/; M. Kirschenbaum, ed., *Image-Based Humanities Computing*: Special issue of *Computers and the Humanities* 36, 3 (2002).

[28] S. Sinclair, S. Ruecker, and M. Radzikowska, 'Information Visualization for Humanities Scholars', in K. M. Price and R. Siemens, eds., *Literary Studies in the Digital Age An Evolving Anthology*, (New York: MLA Commons, Modern Language Association of America, 2013), https://dlsanthology.commons.mla.org/information-visualization-for-humanities-scholars/.

[29] R. Ferguson, 'Learning analytics: drivers, developments and challenges', *International Journal of Technology Enhanced Learning (IJTEL)*, 4, 5/6 (2012), 304–317. G. Siemens,

'Learning Analytics: The Emergence of a Discipline', *American Behavioral Scientist,* 57,10 (2013), 1380–1400.

[30] Siemens, 'Learning Analytics', 1380–1400.

[31] Siemens, G., Baker, R.S.J.d. (2012) Learning Analytics and Educational Data Mining: Towards Communication and Collaboration. Proceedings of the 2nd International Conference on Learning Analytics and Knowledge,

[32] M. Perloff, *Differentials: Poetry, Poetics, Pedagogy*, (Tuscaloosa: U of Alabama P, 2004).

[33] T. Clement, 'Text Analysis, Data Mining, and Visualizations in Literary Scholarship', in K. M. Price and R. Siemens, eds., *Literary Studies in the Digital Age An Evolving Anthology,* (New York: MLA Commons, Modern Language Association of America, 2013), https://dlsanthology.commons.mla.org/text-analysis-data-mining-and-visualizations-in-literary-scholarship/.; T. Clement, ' "A Thing Not Beginning or Ending": Using Digital Tools to Distant-Read Gertrude Stein's *The Making of Americans'*, *Literary and Linguistic Computing*, 23, 3 (2008): 361–82.

[34] Drucker, 'Humanistic Theory and Digital Scholarship'.

SEMI-SUPERVISED TEXTUAL ANALYSIS AND HISTORICAL RESEARCH HELPING EACH OTHER: SOME THOUGHTS AND OBSERVATIONS

FEDERICO NANNI, HIRAM KUMPER AND SIMONE PAOLO PONZETTO

Abstract   *Future historians will describe the rise of the World Wide Web as the turning point of their academic profession. As a matter of fact, thanks to an unprecedented amount of digitization projects and to the preservation of born-digital sources, for the first time they have at their disposal a gigantic collection of traces of our past. However, to understand trends and obtain useful insights from these very large amounts of data, historians will need more and more fine-grained techniques. This will be especially true if their objective will turn to hypothesis-testing studies, in order to build arguments by employing their deep in-domain expertise.*

For this reason, we focus our paper on a set of computational techniques, namely semi-supervised computational methods, which could potentially provide us with a methodological turning point for this change. As a matter of fact these approaches, due to their potential of affirming themselves as both knowledge and data driven at the same time, could become a solid alternative to some of the today most employed unsupervised techniques.

However, historians who intend to employ them as evidences for supporting a claim, have to use computational methods not anymore as black boxes but as a series of well known methodological approaches. For this reason, we believe that if developing computational skills will be important for them, a solid background knowledge on the most important data analysis and results evaluation procedures will become far more capital.

International Journal of Humanities and Arts Computing 10.1 (2016): 63–77
DOI: 10.3366/ijhac.2016.0160
© Edinburgh University Press 2016
www.euppublishing.com/journal/ijhac

Keywords: semi-supervised methods; historical studies; data analysis; born-digital archives

I. INTRODUCTION

In December 2010 Google presented a service called 'Google Ngram Viewer'.[1] This tool allows us to look at the occurrence of single words or sentences in specific subsets of the immense corpus digitized by the Google Books project.

A few weeks after, Erez Lieberman Aiden and Jean-Baptiste Michel, team leaders of the prototype Viewer, offered a demonstration of the tool at the annual meeting of the American Historical Association in Boston.[2] In front of around 25 curious historians, they noted the enormous potential of conducting historical research by extracting information from large corpora. In particular, they revealed a way to deal with one of the biggest issues for historians who are exploring large datasets, namely rapidly detecting the distribution of specific words in the corpus.[3]

Interestingly, the development and the functionalities of this tool demonstrate some of the most relevant characteristics of the current interactions between the practice of historical research and the use of computational methods:

> Firstly, no historian has been directly involved in any step of the development of this project.[4] This is particularly significant, given that they would likely be the primary targets of a tool able to process information from a corpus spanning five hundred years. As Aiden and Michel remarked, this is due to two well-known reasons: historians traditionally do not have solid computational skills and they are usually skeptical about the development of quantitative approaches for the analysis of sources.[5]
>
> Secondly, others have noted that the Ngram Viewer offers an over-simplified research tool, which usually leads to general coarse-grained explorative analyses and to few simple historical discoveries.[6]
>
> Finally, the way in which the Ngram Viewer has been presented and identified outside academia as a representative tool of the digital humanities also reveals the growing enthusiasm for methodology studies and big-data driven researches in this community.[7] However, as already remarked, researchers in digital humanities need to bear in mind their long-term purpose, that is to use the computer in order to answer specific and relevant research questions and not simply to build tools.[8]

But while the Ngram Viewer symbolises a current widespread way of employing computational methods for studying historical corpora, namely for data-exploration and general hypothesis-confirmation analyses, we believe that a change is about to come. In fact, in our opinion new generations of historians

64

will need more and more fine-grained techniques to conduct inspections of large datasets. This will be especially true if their objective turns from exploratory analyses to hypothesis-testing studies, in order to build arguments by employing their deep in-domain expertise.

For this reason, we focus here on a set of computational techniques, namely semi-supervised computational methods, which could potentially provide us with a methodological turning point for this change.[9] As a matter of fact these approaches make it possible to actively include the human expert in the computational process. Therefore, due to their potential of affirming themselves as both *knowledge-* and *data-driven* at the same time, they could become a solid alternative to some of the most common unsupervised techniques currently used.

However, historians who intend to employ computational methods as evidence for supporting a claim, have to use them as a series of well known methodological approaches rather than as 'black boxes' whose workings are unknown.[10]

For this reason, if developing computational skills will be important for historians, a solid background knowledge of the most important data analysis and results evaluation procedures will become far more necessary.

Starting from all these assumptions, this paper is organized as follows: firstly, a few basic concepts of machine learning methods are introduced. Then, a diachronic description of the use of computational methods in historical research is presented. Following this, our focus on a specific technique, namely Latent Dirichlet Allocation topic modeling, is defined. Next, the advantages and the consequences of the use of semi-supervised topic modeling approaches on the historian's craft are described. Finally, a future project on the use of these methodological frameworks for the analysis of the different semantic dimensions of specific concepts in a collection of around 1,000 French legal books from the 17th and 18th century is introduced.

Our essay is focused on a precise potentiality of the complex datasets of sources that historians have now at their disposal. This is the possibility of exploiting the results of fine-grained analyses as historical evidence through the combination of specific in-domain research interests and the scientifically correct employment of computational methods. This will help researchers to deal with the abundance of digital materials by extracting precise information from them, and to move from exploratory studies to hypothesis testing analyses. However, now that both large datasets and text mining methods are at our disposal, other challenges are emerging, such as multilingual corpora or the evolution of languages in diachronic extended datasets. In the near future this will raise other issues for the new generations of historians, increasing the need for advanced computational approaches (i.e. specific language models for machine translation) and demanding always more advanced competencies of the humanities researcher.

2. SUPERVISED AND UNSUPERVISED TEXT ANALYSES

Before going into the details of how these methods have previously been employed in historical research and how they could be used in the near future, it is important to clarify a few key concepts in data analysis and machine learning that have already been mentioned in the previous paragraphs.[11] As described earlier, an initial requirement of many historical studies is to identify semantic similarities and recurrent lexical patterns in a collection of documents. In machine learning there are two main different kinds of approaches that allow us to do this.

The first one consists of *supervised* learning methods, which focus on classification tasks. In classification tasks, humans identify a specific property of a subset of elements in the dataset (for example articles about foreign policy in a newspaper archive) and then guide the computer, by means of an algorithm, to learn how to find other elements with that characteristic. This is done by providing the machine with a dataset of labeled examples ('this is an article about foreign policy', 'this is not'), called a 'gold standard', which are described by a set of other 'features' (for instance, the frequency of each word in each document). Moreover, the learning process is typically divided into two main phases, namely: i) a training phase, in which the predictive model is learnt from the labeled data; ii) a testing phase, in which the previously learnt model is applied to unseen, unlabeled data in order to quantity its predictive power, specifically its ability to generalize to data other than the labeled ones seen during training. Additionally, a validation phase can take place to fine-tune the model's parameters for the specific task or domain at hand – e.g., classifying foreign policy articles from newspaper sources, as opposed to websites.

The potential of a good classifier is immense, in that it offers a model that generalizes from labeled to (a potentially very large set of) unlabeled data. However, building such models can also be extremely time-consuming. In fact, researchers not only need a dataset with specific annotated examples to train the classifier but, perhaps even more fundamentally, they need to have extremely clear sense of what they are looking for, since this leads them to define the annotation guidelines and learning task itself. For this reason, it is evident that classification methods are arguably not the most convenient approaches for conducting data exploration in those situations where a researcher sets out to investigate the dataset with no clear goal in mind other than searching for any phenomenon they deem interesting *a posteriori*.

The second class of methods is *unsupervised*, and addresses the problem of clustering. In a nutshell, clustering methods aim at grouping elements from a dataset on the basis of their similarity, as computed from their set of features (for example by looking at patterns in the frequency of words in different documents). This is achieved by computing likenesses across features without relying on labeled examples, unsupervised by humans. Crucially for digital humanities scholars, researchers can study the resulting clusters in order to understand what the (latent) semantic meaning of the similarities between the elements is.

Clustering techniques are extremely useful for analyzing large corpora of unlabeled data (i.e., consisting of 'just text'), since they rapidly offer researchers a tool to get a first idea of their content in a structured way (i.e., as clusters of similar elements, which can be optionally hierarchically arranged by using so-called hierarchical clustering methods). This is primarily because, as they do not require labeled data, they can be applied without having in mind a specific phenomenon or characteristics of the dataset to mine (i.e., learn). However, even if scholars noted their potential, for example by creating serendipity, and different metrics have been proposed for evaluating the number and correctness of these clusters, this is still an extremely challenging task, typically due to the difficulties of interpreting the clusters output by the algorithms.[12]

3. STUDYING THE PAST, IN THE DIGITAL WORLD

The potential of computational methods for the study of primary sources has been a recurrent topic in the humanities. As Thomas remarked, already in 1945 Vannevar Bush, in his famous essay 'As We May Think', pointed out that technology could be the solution that will enable us to manage the abundance of scientific and humanistic data; in his vision the Memex could become an extremely useful instrument for historians.[13] The use of the computer in historical researches consolidated between the Sixties and the Seventies with its application to the analysis of economic and census data. The advent of cliometrics gave birth to a long discussion on the use of the results of quantitative analysis as evidence in the study of the past.[14]

Due in part to this long debate on the application of quantitative methods in historical research and in part to the new potentials of the Web as a platform for the collection, presentation, and dissemination of material, during the Nineties a different research focus emerged in what was already at that time identified as digital history.[15] As Robertson recently pointed out, this specific attention on the more 'communicative aspects' of doing research in the humanities could be recognized as one of the main differences between the ways in which historians have been interpreting the digital turn compared to their colleagues in literary studies over the last twenty years.[16]

However, regardless of whether historians of the 21st Century are interested in employing computational methods for analysis textual documents or not, it is evident that the never-ending increase of digitized and born digital sources is no longer manageable with traditional close reading hermeneutic approaches alone.[17] For this reason, two different activities have consolidated in the digital humanities community during the last decade. On one side digital historians started creating tools in order to help other traditionally trained colleagues in employing computational methods.[18] On the other side, more recently a small but strongly connected community of historians has decided to focus their efforts on teaching the basic of programming languages and the potential of different textual analyses techniques for conducting exploratory studies of their datasets. As Turkel remarked: 'My priority is to help train a generation of programming historians. I acknowledge the wonderful work that my colleagues are doing by presenting history on the Web and by building digital tools for people who can't build their own. I know that the investment of time and energy that programming requires will make sense only for one historian in a hundred'.[19]

a. Computational History

The works conducted by Willam J. Turkel at the University of Western Ontario, with particular attention to his blog 'Digital History Hacks' and his project 'The programming historian', could be identified as a starting point of these digital interactions.[20] Following Turkel's approaches and advice, a group of historians has begun experimenting with these different computational methods to explore large historical corpora.[21] The use of Natural Language Processing and Information Retrieval methods, combined with network analysis techniques and a solid set of visualization tools, are the points around which this new wave of quantitative methods in historiography has consolidated.

During recent years several interesting examples of these interactions between historical research and computational approaches have been presented.[22] In addition, thanks to the collaborations with other digital humanities colleagues (i.e. literary studies researchers and digital archivists), the words 'text mining' and 'distant reading' have become buzzwords of this new trend in digital history. If we were to look more closely at how these techniques have been applied, we could notice that the first objective of the digital humanities researchers has been to show the exploratory potential of these methods and to confirm their accuracy by re-evaluating already well-known historical facts.[23] As we will remark in the next sections, this is due to the unsupervised nature of the specific textual analysis techniques most widely used in historical research (e.g., topic modeling), which do not need (but at the same time cannot obtain benefit from) human supervision and in-domain knowledge during the computational process.

b. Topic modeling

Topic modeling is arguably the most popular text mining technique in digital humanities.[24] Its success is due to its ability to address one of the deepest need of a historian, namely to automatically identify with as little human supervision as possible (none, ideally) a list of topics in a collections of documents, and how these are intertwined with specific document sources in the collection. At a first sight this technique seems to be the methodological future of historical research.

However, as researchers rapidly discovered, working with topic modeling toolboxes is neither easy nor always yielding satisfactory results. First of all, Latent Dirichlet Allocation (LDA - the main topic models algorithm), like other unsupervised techniques, needs to be told in advance the number of topics (resp. clusters) that the researcher is interested in.[25] However, knowing the number of topics is itself a non-trivial issue, which leads researchers to a chicken-and-egg-problem in which they use LDA to find *some* interesting topics, while being required to explicitly state the *exact number* of such topics they are after. Moreover, as this technique looks at the distribution of topics by document, the results will be extremely different in relation to the number of topics chosen.

Thus, topic modeling highlights both advantages and limitations of unsupervised techniques. In fact, the obtained topics are, as others noticed, usually difficult to decode; each of them is presented as a list of words, and being able to identify it with a specific concept generally depends on the intuitions of the researcher.[26]

The first paper on LDA was published in 2003, however before 2010 there were just a few publications on humanities topics where this technique was employed.[27] We could identify a turning point in the digital humanities community between 2011 and 2012, when suddenly a remarkable number of blogposts, online discussions, workshops and then publications been focused on how to deal and employ this technique.[28] As we will describe later, in the same period Owens observed the risks for humanists of using topic modeling results as justification for a theory and in general suggested limiting its use to exploratory studies.[29]

4. SEMI-SUPERVISED TEXTUAL ANALYSIS

Today, if there is something more criticized than the use of quantitative methods in the humanities, this is data-driven research.[30] More specifically, we agree that the practice of employing unsupervised computational approaches to analyse a dataset and then relying on their automatically generated results to build a scholarly argument could reduce the role of the humanist in the research process. This is due to two main reasons: firstly, since even the more technically skilled historian does not have a solid statistical background as computational linguists, computer scientists or other kinds of researchers that currently are implementing these methods; this will consequently limit their understanding of both the techniques and the obtained results.[31] Secondly, because by employing unsupervised techniques, historians will not draw on their background knowledge, and will not directly use these methods for answering specific research questions they have in mind. This is because, since unsupervised methods do not rely on human supervision and are mainly targeted at generating serendipity, they do not, and are not meant to include human feedback to guide the process of model creation.

However, on the other side of the spectrum, supervised classification approaches are particularly time-consuming to build, and their usefulness depends on specific research purposes (i.e., what is the scholar trying to discover by classifying documents in different categories?). Therefore, it is evident that for historians interested in performing more fine-grained explorations, a different computational technique is needed that is able to stake out a middle ground between explicit human supervision and serendipitous searching and exploration; a method that could help the researcher switching from general exploration analyses to more specific ones, from getting a first idea of the contents of a corpus to start evaluating theories by employing her/his domain expertise.

For this purpose, we argue that a series of semi-supervised topic modeling algorithms, adopted in recent years in the fields of machine learning and natural language processing, could also become established research methods in digital history.

The first one is Supervised LDA, originally presented by Mcauliffe and Blei.[32] This method makes it possible to derive distribution of topics by considering a set of labels, each one associated with each document. In their paper the authors note the potential of this method when the prediction of a specific value is the ultimate goal; to this end, they combine movie ratings and text reviews to predict the score of unrated reviews. However, as remarked by Travis Brown, historians could also experiment with this technique, to, for example identify the relation between topics and labels (i.e. to find the most relevant topics for 'economics' articles).[33]

A conceptual extension of this technique is Labeled LDA, developed by Ramage et al.[34] This method makes it possible to highlight the distribution of labeled topics in a set of multi-labeled documents. If we imagine a corpus where every document is described by a set of meta-tags (for example a newspaper archive with articles associated with both 'economics', 'foreign policy', and so on), Labeled LDA will identify the relation between topics, documents and tags, and its output will consist of a list of topics, one for each tag. This, in turn, could be used to identify which part of each document is associated with each tag.

Another relevant approach is Dirichlet-multinomial regression, proposed by Mimno and McCallum.[35] As the authors describe, rather than generating metadata (as for example the ratings in Supervised LDA) or estimating topical densities for metadata elements (as the topics related to metadata, like Labeled LDA), this method learns topic assignments by considering a set of pre-assigned document-features. In their paper the researchers show how authors, paper-citations and date of publications could be useful features of external knowledge to improve the topic model representation on a dataset of academic publications.

Finally, a last method is Seeded LDA.[36] Instead of using a prior set of descriptive labels for each document or topic, as in previous approaches, Seeded LDA offers the possibility of manually defining a list of seed words for the topics the researcher is interested in. Let us imagine, for instance, that we are after a specific topic within the corpus of interest (e.g., news related to the relations between USA and Cuba in a newspaper archive): using Seeded LDA the researcher could guide the topic model in a specific direction, receiving as output the distribution of topics that she/he is interested in.

A thorough comparison of these different semi-supervised topic modeling techniques is beyond the scope of this paper. However, the fact that all methods make it possible to include the human (i.e., the humanities scholar) in the loop (i.e., the learning process) by requiring the expert to provide either labeled meta-data, or a set of initial seed words to guide the topic acquisition process is crucial for out argument. We argue that this last option, in particular, is very attractive for digital historians in that it forces them to explicitly state the lexical components of the specific topics they are after, while requiring a minimal amount of supervision. That is, the scholar has to input a small set of seed words he/she deems important on the basis of her/his expertise, as opposed to merely labeling documents with a pre-compiled set of class labels.

5. HOW DATA BECOMES EVIDENCE

In the previous section we gave a brief overview of different semi-supervised topic modeling techniques, and argued that they could help historians exploit different sources like metadata and seed words, stemming from their *human expertise as scholars*, in order to perform fine-grained exploration analyses.

Topic modeling is a fascinating way of navigating through large corpora, and it could become even more interesting for the researcher by making the tool consider specific labels or seed-words. Regarding this, Owens remarked: 'If you shove a bunch of text through MALLET and see some strange clumps clumping that make you think differently about the sources and go back to work with them, great'.[37] Then, he continues: 'If you aren't using the results of a digital tool as evidence then anything goes'.

In the second sentence Owens perfectly describes the current main problem of digital humanities scholars employing text mining methods. As others already remarked, on the one hand the research community wants to see the humanistic relevance of these analyses, and not only the computational benefits.[38] On the other hand, digital humanists are aware that they cannot present the results of

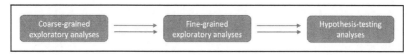

Figure 1. In this figure the methodological framework we suggest for analysing large historical corpora is summarized. Both the in-domain knowledge of the researcher and a solid expertise in data analysis are key components.

their studies as evidence without a solid evaluation of the performance of the methods.

For instance, if the purpose is to detect articles related to a specific subject (i.e. the relations between USA and Cuba), the documents obtained by looking at the distribution of specific (LDA-derived) topics are nothing more than an innovative way of searching through the dataset. Thus, it is important to keep in mind that these documents are not the only articles about the subject, and that maybe they are not even about that specific subject at all – due to the errors in the automatic learning process. Therefore, if we want to transform our data into evidences for supporting a specific argument or for confirming a hypothesis, we always have to evaluate our approach first.

It is interesting to notice that this specific process would sound perfectly ordinary if we were not talking about machine learning methods, computers and algorithms. When a researcher wants to be sure that a viewpoint is correct ('I believe this article is focused on the relations between USA and Cuba'), she/he will ask other colleagues.[39] The process described here is the same: we need human annotations (for example articles marked as 'being focused on the relations between USA and Cuba' or not) in order to confirm that our hypothesis (what the machine is showing to me are articles related to the relations between USA and Cuba) is correct.

Moreover, since humanists are working on extremely specific in-domain research tasks, they cannot rely on Amazon Mechanical Turk annotations as others usually do.[40] For solving this specific issue, they cannot even rely on computer scientists or data mining experts: they need the help of their peers.

Therefore, we believe that future advances in historical research on large corpora will be essentially achieved by *exploiting deep human expertise*, such as that provided by history scholars, as key components *within weakly-supervised computational methods* in two different ways.

In our vision (Fig. 1), a first stage will still consist of exploratory studies, which are extremely useful to develop an initial idea of arbitrary datasets. During this process, both standard LDA and especially the semi-supervised methods presented earlier could be particularly useful, as they will help researchers manage the vastness of digital data at their disposal. Following the exploratory phase, when the interest on a specific phenomenon has been established, we envision researchers moving on and developing models to quantify such phenomenon in text, and creating a gold standard for evaluation based on human ground truth judgments – again, based on input from domain experts, i.e., scholars. During this second part of the study it might be that useful methods for exploratory studies (such as LDA) are not always as helpful when the task is to precisely identify specific phenomena. For this reason, the new generation of historians needs to learn how to employ text classification algorithms and have to become more and more confident with data analysis evaluation procedures.[41] As a matter of fact, these practices have the potential to sustain and improve our comprehension of the past, when dealing with digital sources.

6. CASE STUDY: APPLYING THESE PROCEDURES IN A WELL-DEFINED HISTORICAL RESEARCH

In this final section we describe how we intend to employ the methodological framework presented before in an interdisciplinary research project that, in the near future, will bring together researchers from the Historical Institute and the Data and Web Science Group of the University of Mannheim.

Our cases study will be focused on circa 1,000 legal books from the 17th and 18th century, comprising over 310,000 pages of text. This is of course a large corpus for a historian, but only a small one for current research in computerized text analysis. Therefore, testing computational methods for specific analyses may proof insightful for both disciplines.

These volumes form the 'Juridica' part of a book collection brought to Mannheim by the learned Jesuit François-Joseph Terrasse Desbillons (1711–1798) in the 1770s. They cover a broad variety of legal matters with a special, but not very surprising interests in canon law, and another, little more surprising interest in legal history, or more precisely: the old (French) law.

Based on this corpus, we want to know more about this old French law, the 'ancien droit'. Yet, we do not trace legal institutions, ideas, or regulations. Rather we ask for the fundamental terms that old French law rested upon. These terms lay the conceptual groundwork upon which concrete institutions, rules, and distinctions of legal thinking were built. Hence, they are usually not technical in a stricter sense (i.e. not exclusively legal), or bear multiple semantic dimensions largely depending upon their uses in specific contexts, e.g. terms like *volonté* ('will'), *origin* ('origin'), or *liberté* ('liberty'). We aim to find these terms and their specific contexts, cluster together similar contexts, and weight them against each other, iteratively reaching a broad, yet precise spectrum of their meanings.

Traditionally, dictionaries like these are compiled by domain experts (i.e. historians) by reading large amounts of contemporary texts, and by analysing these texts in what we, broadly speaking, term a 'hermeneutical' fashion. The selection of texts rests upon the researcher and his or her scope of reach, its amount on what he or she can physically read/bear, and its results rest largely on what he or she can find by physically reading either line by line or hastily flipping through the texts. This is not to say that this traditional method cannot or will not lead to fruitful conclusions.[42]

In the end, however, these projects are largely based on the presuppositions of the researcher about what she/he can (or will) actually find in the texts, and which texts will be more likely to give fruitful results. In other words, the researcher predefines both search terms and contexts. Our approach, in contrast, will also start with presuppositions, but iteratively enlarge them by finding both new contexts and probably even new search terms.

It could, for instance, well be that notions of 'will' (*volonté*) and its faculties will be discussed in contexts of compulsion (*contrainte, compulsion, coercition*) without even using a word deriving from *volonté*. Term-based textual analysis will not find such instances, but concept-based analysis will – even in far less obvious examples than the one given here.

As described before, our work will proceed through different steps. In the beginning, coarse-grained exploratory analyses (i.e. using standard LDA) will offer us a general idea of the content of the volumes and their similarities. Then, by combining different weakly-supervised techniques like Supervised LDA and Seeded LDA we will exploit domain expert knowledge to identify the semantic contexts in which these relevant concepts appear and to detect other similar patterns in the corpus. Finally, in order to use the results of these analyses as historical evidences, we will test, compare and improve our methods on a gold standard that it will be built with this specific purpose.

7. CONCLUSIONS

In this paper, we have discussed the applicability of a set of computational techniques for conducting fine-grained analyses on historical corpora. Furthermore, we have remarked the importance of an evaluation step when the data are exploited as evidence to support specific hypotheses. We believe that these practises will allow us to deepen our understanding of historical information embedded in digital data.

ACKNOWLEDGEMENTS

The authors want to thank Laura Dietz (Data and Web Science Group) and Charlotte Colding Smith (Historical Institute) for their precious methodological advice.

END NOTES

[1] https://books.google.com/ngrams; all the URLs mentioned in this research were lastly checked on November 13th 2015.

2 J.B. Michel et al., 'Quantitative analysis of culture using millions of digitized books', *Science*, 331.6014 (2011), 176–182; A. Grafton. 'Loneliness and Freedom', *Perspectives on History*, online edition, March 2011, http://www.historians.org/publications-and-directories/perspectives-on-history/march-2011/loneliness-and-freedom.

3 G. Crane, 'What do you do with a million books?', *D-Lib magazine*, 12.3 (2006).

4 Grafton, 'Loneliness and Freedom'.

5 See: http:// www . culturomics . org / Resources / faq / thoughts - clarifications - on - grafton-s-loneliness-and-freedom; F. Gibbs and T. Owens, 'The hermeneutics of data and historical writing', in J. Dougherty and K. Nawrotzki ed., *Writing History in the Digital Age* (Ann Arbor, MI, 2013).

6 D. Cohen, 'Initial Thoughts on the Google Books Ngram Viewer and Datasets', *Dan Cohen's Digital Humanities Blog,* 19/10/2010, http://www.dancohen.org/2010/12/19/initial-thoughts-on-the-google-books-ngram-viewer-and-datasets/.

7 See the answer to 'How does this relate to 'humanities computing' and 'digital humanities'?' in Culturomics FAQ section: http://www.culturomics.org/Resources/faq; C. S. Fisher, 'Digital Humanities, Big Data, and Ngrams, Boston Review, 20/06/2013, http://www. bostonreview.net/blog/digital-humanities-big-data-and-ngrams; C. Blevins, 'The Perpetual Sunrise of Methodology', 05/01/2015, http://www.cameronblevins.org/posts/perpetual-sunrise-methodology/

8 I. Gregory, 'Challenges and opportunities for digital history', *Frontiers in Digital Humanities,* 1 (2014); M. Thaller, 'Controversies around the Digital Humanities: An Agenda', *Historical Social Research/Historische Sozialforschung* (2012), 7–23.

9 O. Chapelle et al. (edited by), *Semi-Supervised Learning* (Cambridge, MA, 2006).

10 T. Owens, 'Discovery and justification are different: Notes on science-ing the humanities', 19/11/2012, http://www.trevorowens.org/2012/11/discovery-and-justification-are-different-notes-on-sciencing-the-humanities/; D. Sculley and B. M. Pasanek. 'Meaning and mining: the impact of implicit assumptions in data mining for the humanities', *Literary and Linguistic Computing,* 23.4 (2008), 409–424.

11 R. S. Michalski, J. G. Carbonell and T. M. Mitchell, *Machine learning: An artificial intelligence approach* (Heidelberg, 1983).

12 E. Alexander et al. 'Serendip: Topic model-driven visual exploration of text corpora', *Proceedings of IEEE Conference on Visual Analytics Science and Technology* (Paris, 2014); M. Steinbach, G. Karypis, and V. Kumar, 'A comparison of document clustering techniques', *KDD workshop on text mining*. 400–1 (2000), 525–526.

13 W. G. Thomas III, 'Computing and the historical imagination', in S. Schreibman, R. Siemens and J. Unsworth, ed., *A companion to digital humanities* (Oxford, 2004), 56–68.

14 D. N. McCloskey, 'The achievements of the cliometric school', *The Journal of Economic History,* 38.01 (1978), 13–28.

15 D. J. Cohen, and R. Rosenzweig. *Digital history: a guide to gathering, preserving, and presenting the past on the web* (Philadelphia, 2006).

16 S. Robertson, *The differences between digital history and digital humanities*, 23/05/2014, http://drstephenrobertson.com/ blogpost/ the-differences-between-digital-history-and-digital-humanities/.

17 S. Graham, I. Milligan and S. Weingart. *The Historian's Macroscope* - working title, Open Draft Version, Autumn 2013, http://themacroscope.org.

18 For example the TAPoR project: http://www.tapor.ca/.

19 In D. J. Cohen et al, 'Interchange: The promise of digital history', *The Journal of American History* (2008), 452–491.

[20] Willam J. Turkel' blog: http://digitalhistoryhacks.blogspot.com/; The Programming Historian: http://programminghistorian.org/.

[21] For example, I. Milligan, 'Mining the 'Internet Graveyard': Rethinking the Historians' Toolkit', *Journal of the Canadian Historical Association/Revue de la Société historique du Canada,* 23.2 (2012), 21–64.

[22] For instance, C. Blevins, 'Space, Nation, and the Triumph of Region: A View of the World from Houston', *Journal of American History,* 101.1 (2014), 122–147 and M. Kaufman, 'Everything on Paper Will Be Used Against Me: Quantifying Kissinger', 2014, http://blog.quantifyingkissinger.com/.

[23] For example, C. Au Yeung and A. Jatowt. 'Studying how the past is remembered: towards computational history through large scale text mining', *Proceedings of the 20th ACM international conference on Information and knowledge management* (Glasgow, 2011).

[24] E. Meeks and S. Weingart, 'The digital humanities contribution to topic modeling', *Journal of Digital Humanities,* 2.1 (2012), 1–6.

[25] D. M. Blei, A. Y. Ng and M. I. Jordan, 'Latent dirichlet allocation', *the Journal of machine Learning research,* 3 (2003), 993–1022.

[26] J. Chang et al., 'Reading tea leaves: How humans interpret topic models', *Advances in neural information processing systems,* 2009.

[27] R. Brauer, M. Dymitrow and M. Fridlund, 'The digital shaping of humanities research: The emergence of Topic Modeling within historical studies', *Enacting Futures: DASTS 2014* (Roskilde, 2014).

[28] T. Underwood, 'Topic modeling made just simple enough', *The Stone and Shell,* 07/04/2012, http://tedunderwood.com/2012/04/07/topic-modeling-made-just-simple-enough/; Storify of the DH Topic Modeling Workshop: https://storify.com/sekleinman/dh-topic-modeling-seminar; Meeks and Weingart, 'The digital humanities contribution to topic modeling'.

[29] Owens, 'Discovery and justification are different: Notes on science-ing the humanities'.

[30] S. Marche, 'Literature is not data: Against digital humanities', *LA Review of Books* (2012); L. Wieseltier, 'Crimes against humanities', *New Republic,* 244.15 (2013), 32–39.

[31] D. Hall, D. Jurafsky and C. D. Manning, 'Studying the history of ideas using topic models', *Proceedings of the conference on empirical methods in natural language processing* (Honolulu, 2008); D. Mimno, 'Computational historiography: Data mining in a century of classics journals', *Journal on Computing and Cultural Heritage,* 5.1 (2012); M. Schich et al., 'A network framework of cultural history', *Science,* 345.6196 (2014), 558–562.

[32] J. D. Mcauliffe, and D. M. Blei, 'Supervised topic models', *Advances in neural information processing systems* (2008).

[33] T. Brown, 'Telling New Stories about our Texts: Next Steps for Topic Modeling in the Humanities', DH2012: Topic Modeling the Past, http://rlskoeser.github.io/2012/08/10/dh2012-topic-modeling-past/

[34] D. Ramage et al., 'Labeled LDA: A supervised topic model for credit attribution in multi-labeled corpora', *Proceedings of the 2009 Conference on Empirical Methods in Natural Language Processing* (Singapore, 2009).

[35] D. Mimno and A. McCallum 'Topic models conditioned on arbitrary features with Dirichlet multinomial regression', *Uncertainty in Artificial Intelligence,* 2008.

[36] J. Jagarlamudi, H. Daumé III and R. Udupa, 'Incorporating lexical priors into topic models', *Proceedings of the 13th Conference of the European Chapter of the Association for Computational Linguistics* (Avignon, 2012).

[37] Owens, 'Discovery and justification are different: Notes on science-ing the humanities'.

[38] M. Thaller, 'Controversies around the Digital Humanities: An Agenda'.

[39] The examples presented here describe an over simplified case study. However, the complexity of the evaluation process can easily be shown by turning to more complex, realistic tasks like, for example, to identify how the different meanings of 'will' evolve within a reasonably sized historical corpus.

[40] In computational linguistics and natural language processing during last decade the use of human non-expert annotators for the construction of labeled datasets has become an established practice. To know more about the online labor market Amazon Mechanical Turk: https:// www.mturk.com/mturk/welcome.

[41] F. Sebastiani, 'Machine learning in automated text categorization', *ACM computing surveys,* 34.1 (2002), 1–47.

[42] For example R. Koselleck, W. Conze and O. Brunner ed. by, *Geschichtliche Grundbegriffe,* 8 vols. (Stuttgart, 1972–1997) and R. Rolf, E. Schmitt, and H. J. Lüsebrinck, *Handbuch politisch-sozialer Grundbegriffe in Frankreich, 1680–1820* (Berlin et al, 1985ff).

LOST IN THE INFINITE ARCHIVE: THE PROMISE AND PITFALLS OF WEB ARCHIVES

IAN MILLIGAN

Abstract *Contemporary and future historians need to grapple with and confront the challenges posed by web archives. These large collections of material, accessed either through the Internet Archive's Wayback Machine or through other computational methods, represent both a challenge and an opportunity to historians. Through these collections, we have the potential to access the voices of millions of non-elite individuals (recognizing of course the cleavages in both Web access as well as method of access). To put this in perspective, the Old Bailey Online currently describes its monumental holdings of 197,745 trials between 1674 and 1913 as the "largest body of texts detailing the lives of non-elite people ever published." GeoCities.com, a platform for everyday web publishing in the mid-to-late 1990s and early 2000s, amounted to over thirty-eight million individual webpages. Historians will have access, in some form, to millions of pages: written by everyday people of various classes, genders, ethnicities, and ages. While the Web was not a perfect democracy by any means – it was and is unevenly accessed across each of those categories – this still represents a massive collection of non-elite speech.*

Yet a figure like thirty-eight million webpages is both a blessing and a curse. We cannot read every website, and must instead rely upon discovery tools to find the information that we need. Yet these tools largely do not exist for web archives, or are in a very early state of development: what will they look like? What information do historians want to access? We cannot simply map over web tools optimized for discovering current information through online searches or metadata analysis. We need to find information that mattered at the time, to diverse and very large communities. Furthermore, web pages cannot be viewed in isolation, outside of the networks that they inhabited. In theory, amongst corpuses of millions of pages, researchers can find whatever they want

International Journal of Humanities and Arts Computing 10.1 (2016): 78–94
DOI: 10.3366/ijhac.2016.0161
© Edinburgh University Press 2016
www.euppublishing.com/journal/ijhac

to confirm. The trick is situating it into a larger social and cultural context: is it representative? Unique?

In this paper, "Lost in the Infinite Archive," I explore what the future of digital methods for historians will be when they need to explore web archives. Historical research of periods beginning in the mid-1990s will need to use web archives, and right now we are not ready. This article draws on first-hand research with the Internet Archive and Archive-It web archiving teams. It draws upon three exhaustive datasets: the large Web ARChive (WARC) files that make up Wide Web Scrapes of the Web; the metadata-intensive WAT files that provide networked contextual information; and the lifted-straight-from-the-web guerilla archives generated by groups like Archive Team. Through these case studies, we can see – hands-on – what richness and potentials lie in these new cultural records, and what approaches we may need to adopt. It helps underscore the need to have humanists involved at this early, crucial stage.

Keywords: archive; world wide web; historical studies; webscraping; digital history

The Web is having a dramatic impact on how we research and understand the recent past. Historians, who have long laboured under conditions of source scarcity – we wish we had more information about the past, but it was not recorded or preserved – are now confronted with primary sources on a scale that defies both conventional methodologies and standard computational methods.[1] Web archives offer profound promise. Take a comparative example. The Old Bailey Online describes its holdings of 197,745 trials between 1674 and 1913 as the 'largest body of texts detailing the lives of non-elite people ever published'.[2] The web archive of GeoCities, a platform for web publishing that operated from the mid-1990s to the early 2000s, amounts to over 38 million pages. Eventually, historians will have access to billions of such sources written by people of various classes, genders, ethnicities, and ages. While the World Wide Web is not a perfect democracy, by any means and any of the categories listed above, it still represents a massive shift. As a result, web archives exemplify this conundrum and represent challenge as well as opportunity.

What information do we want to access? How was the information collected? How do national boundaries intersect with the realm of the Internet? What are the implications of working with such large archives, collected without the informed consent or even knowledge of the overwhelming majority of contributors? These are pressing concerns. For the most part, historians cannot write histories of the 1990s unless they use web archives: with them, military historians will have access to the voices of rank-and-file soldiers on discussion boards; political historians, to blogs, the cut and thrust of websites, electoral commentary and beyond; and of course, social and cultural historians, to the voices of the people on a scale never before possible.

The stakes are high. If we do not come to grasps with web archives, the histories that we write will be fundamentally flawed. Imagine a history of the late 1990s or early 2000s that draws primarily on print newspapers, ignoring the revolution in communications technology that fundamentally affected how people share, interact, and leave historical traces behind. Yet even as we use web archives, we need to be cognizant of their functionalities, strengths, and weaknesses: we need to begin to theorize and educate ourselves about them, just as historians have been cognizant of analog archives since the cultural turn. As new discovery methods for finding information in web archives begin to appear, historians need to be ready to participate; otherwise we might not know why one particular response is number one, versus number one million.

The sheer amount of social, cultural, and political information generated and presented almost every day within the web archive since the Internet Archive began collecting in 1996 represents a complex data set that will fundamentally reshape the historical profession. We need to be ready.

ON COMPLEX DATA SETS: THREE DIFFERENT EXAMPLES

This is not an abstract concern: the history of the 1990s will be written soon. While there is no common rule for when a topic becomes 'history,' it took less than 30 years after the tumultuous year of 1968 for a varied, developed, and contentious North American historiography to appear on the topic of life in the 1960s.[3] Carrying out 'recent histories,' be they of the 1970s or of events only a few years ago, brings with them a host of methodological issues from a lack of historiography, historical participants who can 'talk back,' and issues of copyright and privacy.[4] The year 2021 will mark the 30th anniversary of the creation of the first publicly accessible website. Just as media, government, and business radically transformed their practices in the 1990s, historians must do so as well to analyze this information. 'New media' is not that new anymore.

Historians run very real risks if they are not prepared. Currently, the main way to access the archived Web is through the Wayback Machine, most notably associated with the Internet Archive. The Internet Archive emerged out of a concern around a 'digital dark age' in the mid-1990s, where rapid technological evolution led to fears around whether our heritage was being preserved. Responding to this, Internet entrepreneur Brewster Kahle founded the Internet Archive in June 1996, which began to rapidly grow their web archive collection. They did so by sending 'web crawlers,' automated software programs, out into the Web to download webpages that they found. This crawling process meant that depending on how the Web developed and the limits placed on a crawler, the crawler could indefinitely collect – generating an infinite archive.[5]

While the Internet Archive was collecting data from 1996 onwards, the next step was to make it accessible to researchers. In 2001, they launched the still-dominant form of interacting with web archives: the Wayback Machine. You can try it yourself at http://archive.org/web. It is limited. A user needs to know the exact Uniform Resource Locator (URL) that they are looking for: a website like http://www.geocities.com/enchantedforest/1008/index.html, for example. The page is then retrieved from the web archive and displayed. If you know the URL of the page you are interested in, and only want to read a few, the Wayback Machine works by generating facsimiles of those pages. They are not perfect, as they may not collect embedded images, or might grab them at slightly different times (to avoid overloading any single server, the crawler might download the text of a website and then the image a few hours or even days later; this can lead to the storing of websites that never existed in the first place).[6] Beyond technical issues, it is difficult to find documents with the Wayback Machine unless you know the URL that you want to view.

This latter shortcoming disqualifies it as a serious research tool unless it is paired with a search engine of some kind. Historians are used to full-text search interfaces. However, imagine conducting research through date-ordered keyword search results, carried out on billions of sites. It would produce an outcome similar to the current methods by which historians search digitized newspapers.[7] In the absence of contextual information about the results found, they can be useless. It is possible to find almost anything you want within 38 million web pages. I can find evidence on any matter of topics that advances one particular argument or interpretation. Without the contextual information provided by the archive itself, we can be misled.

Three case studies can help us better understand the questions, possibilities, and challenges facing historians as we enter this archival territory. The first is the Wide Web Scrape, a compilation of billions of objects collected by the Internet Archive between 9 March and 23 December 2011. Next, I explore work that I have been doing with a collection of political websites created between 2005 and 2015. Finally, I explore the GeoCities end-of-life torrent, to get at the heart of ethical challenges.

Together, these studies suggest a path forward for historians. Those of us who use web archives do not need to become programmers, but do need to become aware of basic Web concepts: an understanding of what metadata is, how the Web works, what a hyperlink is, and basic definitional concepts such as URLs. Beyond this, however, is the crucial dimension of algorithmic awareness. When we query archives, we need to know why some results are coming to the top and others at the bottom. If we turn our research over to black boxes, the results that come from them can reaffirm biases: websites belonging to the powerful, for example, rather than the marginalized voices we might want to explore and consider. The decisions that we as historians make now will have profound effects as tools begin to be developed to access web archives.

As a data set, the Wide Web Scrape is exhaustive, transcending national borders. The 2,713,676,341 item captures – websites, images, PDFs, Microsoft Word documents, and so forth – are stored across 85,570 WebARChive (WARC) files.[8] The WARC file format, which is certified by the International Standards Organization, preserves web-archived information in a concatenated form.[9] Generated by the Internet Archive, these files also serve as a good introduction to the geographic challenges of web archives: historians tend towards geographic boundaries, but these archives can transcend them. WARC files are an abundant resource, but that abundance is double edged.

As a Canadian historian looking for a relatively circumscribed corpus, I decided to focus on the Canadian Web, or *websphere*, as best I could. The 'Canadian Web', is however, intrinsically a misnomer. The Web does not work within national boundaries. It is a global network, transcending traditional geopolitical barriers (local fissures still appear, as seen in 'this video is not available in your country' messages).[10] The Internet Archive exploits the Web's borderless nature in their global crawling of material in a way national domain crawls by national institutions cannot. From Denmark to Britain, researchers collecting and studying national webspheres have taken different approaches. Some, such as the Danish NetLab, have confined their studies to national top-level domains (.dk).[11] Others, such as the British Library's born-digital legal deposit scheme, use algorithms and human intervention to find British sites outside of the .uk domain.

What does the data collected along the lines of a national websphere – a top-level domain such as .ca – look like? While all archival records are only as useful as the discovery tools that accompany them – a misfiled box in a conventional archive might as well not exist – the size of these collections elude traditional curation. From the holdings of the Wide Web Scrape, we examined the CDX files (akin to archival finding aids which contain information about the records found within archival boxes), and which can be measured in gigabytes rather than terabytes. They contain millions of lines of text like:

ca,yorku,justlabour)/ 20110714073726 http://www.justlabour.yorku.ca/text/ html 302 3I42H3S6NNFQ2MSVX7XZKYAYSCX5QBYJ http://www.just labour.yorku.ca/index.php?page=toc&volume=16-462   880654831WIDE-20110714062831-crawl416/WIDE-20110714070859-02373.warc.gz

From this, we can learn a few things: in this case, we learn that the record is justlabour.yorku.ca, collected on 14 July 2011 at 7:37 GMT. It redirected (HTML code 302) to the table of contents for volume 16. If you visit justlabour.yorku.ca today, you'll be redirected to a more recent issue. CDX files help us find specific records. Accordingly, I used them to download a sample of 622,365 .ca URLs.

Working with this data set was an interesting window into the choices historians need to make when they work with large data sets from the Web. Derived data – plain text, named entities (discussed later), extracted links, hyperlinks with anchor text – can be useful. Yet at every stage they present historians with questions. Some extracted hyperlinks will be relative – that is, /destination.html rather than http://www.history.ca/destination.html. Should they be reclassified if we want to make a chart of all the hyperlinks connecting different websites, and at what stage? To create plain text files, we use the warcbase platform.[12] I was able to run textual analysis, extract location data, postal codes, and names of people, and explore the topics people were discussing. This method had the downside, however, of removing images, backgrounds, and layouts, meaning that text is taken out of context. While the size of the data sets under discussion mitigates this to some extent, we are still profoundly altering sources.

There were three promising ways to query this data, each of which sheds light on various web archival challenges: keywords, named entity recognition (which finds entities like locations and names within text), and hyperlink structures. To search a large body of material with keywords, the Apache Solr search engine is ideal. It can index material and respond to queries from a number of front-ends that can run locally on a computer.[13] The United Kingdom's Web Archive, for example, uses a custom front-end Solr portal that provides full-text search access to their collections.[14] One view prompts you to enter a query, and to then subsequently see the relative frequency of that term rise and fall over time (how often was the word 'nationalize' used in 2006, for example, compared to 2012). With specific queries, this search approach works well. Yet on a broad scale, when looking for cultural trends, more context is necessary.

The most promising keyword approach to my data set was clustering, which takes a set of documents and groups them. If a web collection contained websites about cats, dogs, and pigs, the algorithm might cluster the cat sites together. Conversely, it might find another characteristic – the ages of the authors, perhaps – and cluster them that way. There are several different algorithms to choose from, although in my experience the Lingo clustering algorithm provides the best results (See Fig. 1).[15]

The free Carrot2 front end (http://project.carrot2.org/), which interfaces easily with a Solr database, is the most useful. From a query for 'children', we see that this sample of 622,365 websites contains pages relating to child health, health

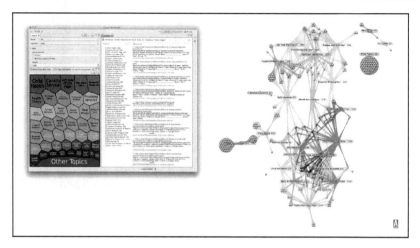

Figure 1. Carrot2 clustering workbench results.

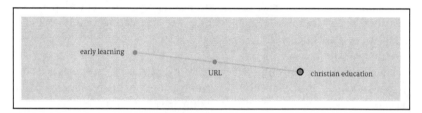

Figure 2. Example of connected clusters.

centres, service providers, public health, educational services, and consumer products such as Tylenol. Clicking on the graphical representation brings the user to a list of documents, and another click brings up an individual document. The image on the right is the graphical representation of overlapping clusters, such as the simplified Figure 2.

If a dot is connected to two clusters, it belongs to both. These connections can provide a rough sense of how representative things are: there are many websites about breastfeeding, for example, but not many about Christian early childhood education institutions. More importantly, it is possible to isolate a corpus to study. Used jointly, the Solr database and Carrot2 front end help transcend the Wayback Machine's limitations.

The main drawback with this approach is the need to know what you are looking for. Extracting commonly mentioned locations can be fruitful, as in Figure 3.

Extracted using a combination of Stanford Named Entity Recognition (NER), Google Maps API, and verification by student research assistants, this

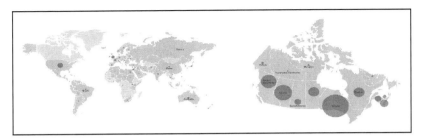

Figure 3. Countries (other than Canada) mentioned in .ca top-level domain sample (left); Canadian provinces mentioned (right).

process found location names – for example, 'Toronto' or 'Johannesburg' – and geolocated them by assigning coordinates. While longitudinal data will be more useful, allowing us to see how various locations changed over time, at this point we can see the attention paid towards Canadian trading partners and the complete absence of attention towards sub-Saharan Africa. Within Canada, Québec is overrepresented vis-à-vis the province of Ontario.

Web-wide scrapes represent the dream of social history: a massive documentary record of the lives of everyday people, their personal websites, small businesses, labour unions, community groups, and so forth. Yet the value of this information is balanced by the sheer size and complexity of these data sets. Web-wide scrapes are one extreme of what we can do with web archives: exploring a massive record of human activity, collected on a previously unimaginable scale.

ARCHIVE-IT POLITICAL COLLECTIONS: AN IDEAL SIZE?

Web-wide scrapes are time consuming and expensive to work with. Recognizing this, web archivists have begun to move towards more accessible data sets that bridge the gap between the lightweight CDX file and the heavy-duty WARC file (both of which we have seen in the preceding section). In this section, I argue that while our first inclination, as with the Wide Web Scrape, might be to go right to the content, more fruitful historical information can be found within the metadata.

Archive-It, a web archiving subscription service provided by the Internet Archive for universities and other institutions, recently piloted their research services portal. It provides access to Web Archive Transformation, or WAT, files: a happy medium between CDXs and WARCs. These provide rich metadata: everything that a CDX has, plus metatext about the website, the title, and the links and anchor text from each site. They are essentially the WARCs sans content, making them much smaller.

Table 1. Hyperlink Example.

Source	Target	Weight (number of links)
Conservative.ca	Liberal.ca	10
Liberal.ca	NDP.ca	10

Beginning a decade ago, the University of Toronto Library (UTL) has put together thematic web collections with Archive-It. One of their major collections is about Canadian political parties and political interest groups, collected quarterly since 2005. Canada has seen pivotal changes within its political sphere over the last ten years, between 2005 and 2015: an arguable militarization of Canadian society, the transition from the 'natural governing party' of the centrist Liberal Party of Canada to the Conservative Party of Canada (and back in late 2015), as well as major policy changes on foreign policy, science policy, and climate change.[16] Given these critical shifts, it is surprising on one level that UTL's collection was not used more – the collection, for example, has never been cited before we began to work with it. On another level, however, it is unsurprising: the current portal to work with the collection at https://archive-it.org/collections/227 has only a very basic search function. It was only by reaching out to librarians at UTL and the Internet Archive that I was able to get the files and begin to explore what we could actually do with them. Ultimately, it became clear that metadata was just as – and in many cases more – useful than the content itself (we ended up providing access to the content through http://webarchives.ca, an implementation of the British Library's Shine frontend).

By using either the Internet Archive's web analysis workshop or warcbase, a web archiving platform, we can extract links the WAT files in this collection by domain.[17] The results look similar to the example in Table 1.

In this case, we can see that among the sub-sites that make up the Conservative Party's website there are ten links to websites within the liberal.ca domain, and vice versa. This sort of data needs to be used with caution, however: one strategic, high-profile link to a website might have more impact than lots of smaller links. For example, a single link on the front page of a political party's website has far greater impact than hundreds of links contained in the footers of biographical statements. We call this the 'weight' because it dictates how much emphasis should be put on the lines that connect various nodes.

This data can be useful on a large scale. Consider Figure 4, which visualizes the external links stemming from and between the websites of Canada's three main political parties. Each line, or edge, represents a hyperlink between domains (or nodes).

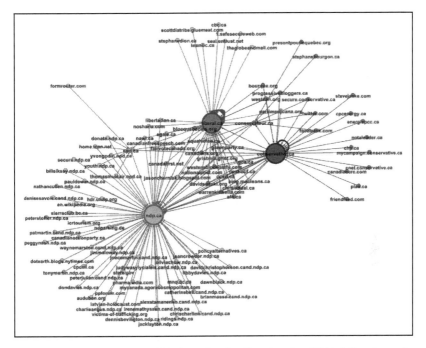

Figure 4. Three major political parties in Canada, the NDP, Liberals, and Conservatives, 2005–2009.

Above, we can see which pages only link to the left-leaning New Democratic Party (NDP or ndp.ca), those that link only to the centrist Liberals (liberal.ca) in the top, and those that only connect to and from the right-wing Conservative Party at right. In the middle are the websites that either link to all three parties or to just two of the three (to the left and right of the Liberal node, respectively). Even from this graph we can see that while many groups link to only the Liberals and the NDP, or to the Liberals and the Conservatives, few link just to the NDP and the Conservatives.

By taking quarterly slices of the data, we can also use metadata to identify the broad contours of a narrative as in Figure 5.

We can see that several entities link to all three parties, such as the environmentalist davidsuzuki.org or the Assembly of First Nations (afn.ca), and we can also see how all of the organizations linked to each other. The Liberal Party was then in power and was under attack by both the opposition parties. In particular, the left-leaning NDP linked hundreds of times to their ideologically close cousins, the centrist Liberals, as part of their electoral attacks, ignoring the

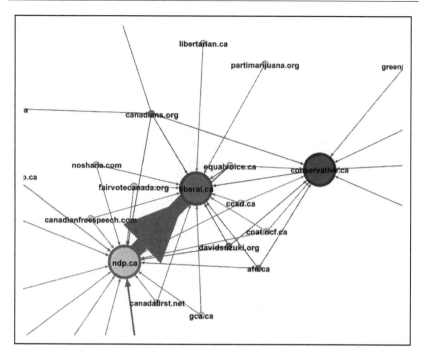

Figure 5. Link structures during the lead-up to the 2006 federal election.

right-leaning Conservative Party in the process. Link metadata illuminates more than a close reading of an individual website would.

We can also find sections of this collection that link far more to themselves than to other parts. These divisions lend themselves well to specific extraction. Consulting the UTL's entire collection via WARC files may be too difficult, but link analysis can tell us what to download. One experiment proved interesting. I took the two main political parties, the Liberals and Conservatives, over the period of study and (relying solely on links) found the communities that grew out of their party websites. The results were interesting: liberal.ca was in the same community as interest groups such as the National Association of Women and Law and media organizations such as *Maclean's* magazine and the Canadian Broadcasting Corporation. Most interestingly, the left-wing New Democratic Party of Canada appeared in the same community. For the Conservatives, they were grouped with many cabinet ministers' pages, but also with groups such as Consumers First, which fought for price parity between Canada and America.

By extracting some of these pages and topic modeling the results, we can confirm existing narratives and raise new questions. Topic modeling finds 'topics' in text. For example, imagine that I am writing about women in a male-dominated labour movement. When I write about the women, I use words like 'femininity', 'equity', 'differential', and 'women'. Men: masculinity', 'wildcat', or 'foremen'. In this thought experiment, imagine I am drawing these words from buckets full of slips of paper. Topic modeling reverses that process, putting those words back into the bucket and telling me what is in it. It is a quick way to get a sense of what might be happening in a large body of text.[18]

Taking the link community that appeared around political parties, we were able to find topics most closely connected to them. In December 2014, the Liberals were highlighting cuts to social programs, issues of mental health, municipal issues, housing, and their new leader, Justin Trudeau (now, as of October 2015, the new Prime Minister of Canada). The Conservatives: Ukraine, the economy, family and senior issues, and the high-profile stimulus-based Economic Action Plan. For 2006, the results were surprising. The Liberals: community questions, electoral topics (given the federal election), universities, human rights, childcare support, and northern issues. The Conservatives: some education and governance topics, but notably, several relating to Canada's aboriginal population. While the Liberals had advanced a comprehensive piece of legislation designed to improve the conditions of Canada's aboriginal population, Conservative interest in the topic was surprising: perhaps it reflects the Conservative opposition to it? As one commenter on an earlier draft suggested, it may represent the influence of key advisors, one of whom was a leading Conservative scholar of native-newcomer relations. Questions are raised, suggesting promise in marrying content and metadata in such a manner.

A PLACE OF THEIR OWN: EXPLORING THE ETHICAL MINEFIELD OF GEOCITIES

In general, the sheer scale of distantly reading millions of websites or exploring the public record of political parties has kept us in the previous cases removed from everyday individuals. As the Web became mainstream in the mid-to-late 1990s, GeoCities played a critical role. For the first time, users could create their own web pages without learning HTML or FTP. On sites like GeoCities, they could become part of part of virtual communities, held together by volunteers, neighbourhood watches, web rings, and guestbooks. Even though in 1999 GeoCities was perhaps the third most popular website in existence, Yahoo! deleted it in 2009. Dedicated teams of Internet archivists, such as Archive Team (http://archiveteam.org), created the web archive that we can use today. It is large: at its peak, GeoCities had around 38 million pages.

GeoCities began in late 1994 as a service predicated on geospatial metaphors and giving voices to those who 'had not had an equal voice in society'.[19] Users could easily create new sites within an existing GeoCities community, such as the Enchanted Forest for children or Area 51 for science fiction fans. They received an 'address' based on their neighbourhood: www.geocities.com/ EnchantedForest/1005/index.html. In an era when the Web was understood as a new 'frontier', this claim to an actual address resonated.[20] User numbers skyrocketed, from 1,400 in July 1995 to 100,000 by August 1996 and a million by October 1997.

I have been exploring the question of how community was created and enacted there. A significant minority of users threw themselves into the site. When a user arrived to create their site, they had to choose where to live: a small 'cottage' in the Enchanted Forest, perhaps, or a 'tent' in Pentagon.[21] Reminders exhorted them to fit into the site's theme, reach out to neighbours, and crucially – in a move reminiscent of the American 1862 *Homestead Act* – 'move in' and improve their property within a week.[22] Some users became community leaders, welcoming new arrivals and teaching them the ropes. An awards economy boomed, with users creating their own awards and giving them to other sites. They visited each other's guestbooks. Messages are disproportionately from GeoCities users rather than visitors from outside. This community structure persisted until 1999, when Yahoo! bought GeoCities and turned it into a conventional web host.

Like in the previous section, we can explore neighbourhoods with topic modelling. We can see topics in the Enchanted Forest about parties, friends, soldiers and children's characters such as Pingu. In Heartland, topics relating to family, church, and genealogy appear, and in the LGBT-focused WestHollywood, the focus is on gender, transgender issues, and fighting against hate crimes. Over time, the topics discussed in some neighbourhoods changed. Pentagon moved beyond being a hub for deployed and constantly moving service people towards serving as a forum for political discussions and military history. Heartland came to advance a vision of family focused on Christianity and genealogy. These findings demonstrate that neighbourhoods both shaped and were shaped by user contributions.

How did this come to be? By extracting links, we can begin to find the central nodes that dozens or even hundreds of other websites linked to, as well as the web of connections that held everybody together. This gives us a few hundred websites per neighbourhood to investigate: the community leaders who received kudos from their members, sites that accumulated awards, those with active guestbooks. These factors produced many hyperlinks, both in and out, making these sites critical nodes.

Websites like GeoCities raise ethical questions. Unlike in our previous case studies, which dealt with institutional websites, in GeoCities we are dealing with largely personal websites from over a decade ago. The majority of these people almost certainly did not create these sites with a future historian in mind, nor are they likely to be aware that their sites live on within the Internet Archive or the Archive Team torrent. They did not give consent to the archiving of their sites, nor did they have access to a robots.txt file that could have changed access parameters (see http://archive.org/about/exclude.php). Indeed, unless they remember their URL, users cannot see if their sites were archived in order to pursue their removal from the archive. Traditional archival collections often have restrictions: donor requests, privacy legislation, or the protection of personal information on medical, financial, or other grounds. While historians have ethical responsibilities at all times, in many cases the onus of making a collection available and accessible lies with institutions. Oral historians, on the other hand, operate outside traditional institutions, instead working in the personal spaces of their interviewees. Institutional review boards, committees that oversee how human subjects are used in research within most North American contexts, govern their work. While none of the above is simple, it is well-travelled ground. Where do web archives fall between these poles?

Strictly speaking, as we generally treat websites as 'publications', it is legal to quote from tweets, blogs, websites, and so forth. Legal does not equal ethical, though. As Aaron Bady notes, 'The act of linking or quoting someone who does not regard their twitter as public is only ethically fine if we regard the law as trumping the ethics of consent.'[23] We need to consider user privacy expectations, which is at the heart of the distinction between a political candidate's site and a GeoCities homestead. This is not to treat users as dupes but to recognize that somebody posting a website in an obscure corner of GeoCities might have an expectation of privacy: many of these sites would not have been discovered by regular users but are easily discovered by web crawlers methodically crawling a community structure.

We can find guidance from web scholars. danah boyd, a web scholar, notes that students with open Facebook profiles regarded a teacher visiting their page as a breach of privacy, social norms, and etiquette.[24] The Association of Internet Researchers provides guidance that has researchers consider the public or private nature of the website and the differences between dealing with sources *en masse* versus individually.[25] Stine Lomberg has emphasized the importance of distance but also, when exploring content, of considering user expectations of privacy.[26]

Historians need to consider these factors when deciding how to appropriately use this material. Some GeoCities cases bring these questions into perspective. Memorial sites, by people who lost children or other loved ones, are both private and intimate but also have well-travelled guestbooks, often by people who lost loved ones of their own. Other searches bring up pages about suicide or depression. These can only be found thanks to today's modern discovery tools. If a 15-year old wrote to the government with a rant, privacy legislation would excise her or his name; if you find the rant in GeoCities, the name – or their pseudonym (which can sometimes be connected to real names) – would be there. These are resources that would never make it into a traditional archive.

We have power because we can access the blogs, ruminations, and personal moments of literally millions of people that would never before have been accessed – but we need to use this power responsibly. With the Wayback Machine, the lack of full-text search provides some privacy, but as we undertake more computational inquiries historians can uncover things forgotten since their creation. My own take on this question is twofold, drawing on earlier literature: we need to consider the scale at play. Mining a few thousand sites and dealing with – and writing about – people in aggregate presents few privacy concerns, whereas zooming in on a handful of websites and closely reading them does. A website many other sites connect to, a proud prominent view counter in the corner (or other equivalent markers of popularity that have supplanted this now dated approach), a well-travelled guestbook, signals a website of an owner who wanted to be read and encountered, and who conceived of themselves as part of a broader Web of documents. A smaller website addressed to an internal audience, written by a teenager and full of revealing messages and pictures, is a different thing altogether.

GeoCities represents a new kind of primary source: the largely non-commercialized, unfettered thoughts of millions of everyday people in the mid-to-late 1990s, left for historians today. We can learn invaluable things, from the forms online community took on the Web to the opinions and thoughts on a host of social, political, or cultural issues or topics.

CONCLUSIONS

These three disparate web archiving case studies all demonstrate the critical questions that lie at the heart of these new complex data sets. The technical challenges are clear: not enough processing power or computer memory, the need to find access to a computing cluster, and the variety of file formats and types that underlie them. Rather than a narrow-lens pedagogical approach that stresses say the WARC file, historians who want to use these sources – arguably a necessity when undertaking topics in the 1990s and beyond – need to have a flexible understanding of software and standards.

While this article has focused on the research process, further issues will emerge when scholars attempt to publish this type of work. Images, already a sticking point with many publishers, are borrowed, altered, shared, throughout the Web: can one publish a notable image found in a 1996-era web archive if this has no contactable author or even real name? How can we share our research data with each other if we need to worry about digital rights? How do we balance global copyright regimes with the local contexts of journals and academics? At the least, pedagogical training in copyright is needed, as well as advocacy around orphan works and strengthening fair dealing/use.

Despite these challenges and cautions, which need to be heeded as we move forward, I want to return to the original promise articulated at the beginning of this paper. Each of these case studies, from the Wide Web Scrape to the political movements archive to GeoCities, presents promise. They provide more voices from a more diverse body of people, furthering the goals of social historians to write their histories from the bottom up, to move our stories away from the elites and dominant players of society to the everyday. Web archives are not going to have a slight impact on the practice of history: they are going to force a profound shift. We will have more sources than ever before, by people who never could have conceivably reached large audiences or had their words recorded. We should be optimistic, but we need to be prepared.

END NOTES

[1] R. Rosenzweig, 'Scarcity or abundance? preserving the past in a digital era', *American Historical Review*, 108, no. 3 (2003), 735–62.

[2] Old Bailey Online, *The proceedings of the Old Bailey, 1674–1913*, http://www.oldbaileyonline.org/, last accessed 16 June 2015.

[3] For examples from the Canadian context, see C. Levitt, *Children of privilege: student revolt in the sixties: a study of student movements in Canada, the United States, and West Germany* (Toronto, 1984) or D. Owram, *Born at the right time: a history of the baby boom generation* (Toronto, 1997).

[4] An excellent and path-breaking anthology on this topic is C. Potter, R. Romano, eds., *Doing Recent History: On Privacy, Copyright, Video Games, Institutional Review Boards, Activist Scholarship, and History That Talks Back* (Athens, GA, 2012).

[5] No good history of the Internet Archive yet exists, but for more information see D. Gillmor, 'Future Historians Will Rely on Web,' *Philadelphia Inquirer*, September 22, 1996; Internet Archive, 'The Internet Archive: Building an 'Internet Library,'' 20 May 2000, http://web.archive.org/web/20000520003204/http://www.archive.org/; A. Brown, *Archiving Websites: A Practical Guide for Information Management Professionals* (London, 2006); S. Meloan, 'No Way to Run a Culture', *Wired*, February 13, 1998, http://web.archive.org/web/20000619001705/http://www.wired.com/news/culture/0,1284,10301,00.html.

[6] S. G. Ainsworth, M. L. Nelson, and H. Van de Sompel, 'Only One Out of Five Archived Web Pages Existed As Presented,' *Proceedings of the 26th ACM Conference on Hypertext & Social Media*, (New York, NY), 257–66.

[7] I. Milligan, 'Illusionary Order: Online Databases, Optical Character Recognition, and Canadian History, 1997–2010,' *Canadian Historical Review* 94, no. 4 (2013), 540–69.

[8] For more, see Internet Archive, *Wide Crawl started March 2011*, 2012, http://archive.org/details/wide00002, last accessed 16 June 2015; V. Goel, *2011 WIDE Crawl (wide00002)*, 2012, http://archive.org/~vinay/wide/wide-00002.html, last accessed 16 June 2015.

[9] International Standards Organization, *ISO 28500:2009 – Information and documentation – WARC file format*, 2009, http://www.iso.org/iso/catalogue_detail.htm?csnumber=44717, last accessed 16 June 2015.

[10] For more on the history of the Internet, see J. Abbate, *Inventing the Internet* (Cambridge, Mass, 2000); T. Berners-Lee, *Weaving the Web: The Original Design and Ultimate Destiny of the World Wide Web* (San Francisco, 2000); J. Ryan, *A History of the Internet and the Digital Future* (London, 2011). A good overview of how the Internet works can be found in A. Blum, *Tubes: A Journey to the Center of the Internet* (New York, 2013).

[11] N. Brügger, D. Laursen, and J. Nielsen, 'Studying a Nation's Web Domain over Time: Analytical and Methodological Considerations', presented at the International Internet Preservation Consortium 2015, Palo Alto, California, April 27, 2015. http://netpreserve.org/sites/default/.../2015_IIPC-GA_Slides_02_Brugger.pptx, accessed July 27, 2015.

[12] Warcbase is documented at https://github.com/lintool/warcbase/wiki.

[13] Apache Software Foundation, *Apache Lucene – Apache Solr*, accessed 21 August 2013, http://lucene.apache.org/solr/, last accessed 16 June 2015.

[14] UK Web Archive, *Shine application*, http://www.webarchive.org.uk/shine, last accessed 16 June 2015. My sincerest thanks to Andy Jackson and his team for making such an inspirational platform.

[15] S. Osiński, J. Stefanowski, and D. Weiss, 'Lingo: search results clustering algorithm based on singular value decomposition', *Advances in soft computing, intelligent information processing and web mining: proceedings of the International IIS: IIPWM'04 Conference* (Zakopane, Poland, 2004), 359–68, http://www.cs.put.poznan.pl/dweiss/site/publications/download/iipwm-osinski-weiss-stefanowski-2004-lingo.pdf, accessed 27 July 2015.

[16] More information on these shifts can be found in I. McKay and J. Swift, *Warrior Nation: Rebranding Canada in an Age of Anxiety* (Toronto, 2012) and Y. Frenette, 'Conscripting Canada's Past: The Harper Government and the Politics of Memory,' *Canadian Journal of History* 49, no. 1 (2014): 50–65.

[17] V. Goel, *Web archive analysis workshop – Internet research – IA webteam confluence*, https://webarchive.jira.com/wiki/display/Iresearch/Web+Archive+Analysis+Workshop, last accessed 16 June 2015; J. Lin et al, *warcbase*, https://github.com/lintool/warcbase/, last accessed 16 June 2015.

[18] This is a shorter version of the great M. Jockers, 'The LDA Buffet: A Topic Modeling Fable,' *matthewjockers.net*, http://www.matthewjockers.net/macroanalysisbook/lda/, last accessed 5 November 2015.

[19] S. Hansell, 'The neighbourhood business: GeoCities' cyberworld is vibrant, but can it make money?', *New York Times*, 13 July 1998.

[20] F. Turner, *From counterculture to cyberculture: Stewart Brand, the Whole Earth network, and the rise of digital utopianism* (Chicago, 2008).

[21] G. Graham, *The Internet: a philosophical inquiry* (London, 1999), 148.

[22] J. Logie, 'Homestead Acts: rhetoric and property in the American West, and on the World Wide Web', *Rhetoric Society Quarterly* 32, no. 3 (1 July 2002), 33–59.

[23] A. Bady, *#NotAllPublic, Heartburn, Twitter*, 10 June 2014, http://thenewinquiry.com/blogs/zunguzungu/notallpublic-heartburn-twitter/, last accessed 16 June 2015.

[24] d. boyd, *It's complicated: the social lives of networked teens* (New Haven, 2014), 58.

[25] A. Markham and E. Buchanan, *Ethical decision-making and Internet research: recommendations from the AOIR Ethics Working Committee (version 2.0)*, September 2012, http://aoir.org/reports/ethics.pdf, last accessed 16 June 2015.

[26] S. Lomborg, 'Personal Internet archives and ethics', *Research Ethics* 9, no. 1 (1 March 2013), 20–31.

THE WORLD WIDE WEB AS COMPLEX DATA SET: EXPANDING THE DIGITAL HUMANITIES INTO THE TWENTIETH CENTURY AND BEYOND THROUGH INTERNET RESEARCH

MICHAEL L. BLACK

Abstract   *While intellectual property protections effectively frame digital humanities text mining as a field primarily for the study of the nineteenth century, the Internet offers an intriguing object of study for humanists working in later periods. As a complex data source, the World Wide Web presents its own methodological challenges for digital humanists, but lessons learned from projects studying large nineteenth century corpora offer helpful starting points. Complicating matters further, legal and ethical questions surrounding web scraping, or the practice of large scale data retrieval over the Internet, will require humanists to frame their research to distinguish it from commercial and malicious activities. This essay reviews relevant research in the digital humanities and new media studies in order to show how web scraping might contribute to humanities research questions. In addition to recommendations for addressing the complex concerns surrounding web scraping this essay also provides a basic overview of the process and some recommendations for resources.*

Keywords: intellectual property, world wide web, webscraping, text mining, 20th century

I. INTRODUCTION

While the digital humanities benefits from the increasing availability of high-quality data repositories, copyright and other forms of intellectual property

International Journal of Humanities and Arts Computing 10.1 (2016): 95–109
DOI: 10.3366/ijhac.2016.0162
© Edinburgh University Press 2016
www.euppublishing.com/journal/ijhac

protection limit the field largely to the study of pre-twentieth century culture. As a result, scholars working in contemporary periods are limited in their ability to implement digital methodologies and/or are enticed to retrain themselves to study an earlier period.[1] These problems notwithstanding, even scholars who do wish to work with texts available through information services such as HathiTrust or JSTOR's Data for Research program are often required to arrange for secure data storage, a potentially costly and time consuming hurdle. Thus far the primary solution to these problems has been the development of 'non-consumptive' research platforms that provide indirect access to protected data. In this essay, I argue for an alternative solution: the use of born digital content available over the World Wide Web can serve both as one way for scholars of twentieth and twenty-first century culture to participate in the new methodological experimentation of the digital humanities and as a low-cost entry point to data analysis for scholars without significant resources. Using the Internet as a data source has the potential to draw fields like new media studies, software studies, science and technology studies, and Internet history into the digital humanities, while at the same time establishing a scholarly community that is more international in scope than those based around major print data repositories, which continue to rely on cultural categories defined around national identities.[2]

Approaching the Internet as a cultural data source can provide digital humanities scholars with a wide range of information on both historic and contemporary cultural phenomena. Many media forms such as textual novels, graphic novels, games, television, and film now have an extended web presence,[3] and as a result the Internet is quickly becoming a site where people continually respond to and debate the importance of cultural processes.[4] Furthermore, because web conversations are by default largely textual, the Internet continually documents what Paul Prior refers to as the 'literate activity' that occurs around texts both popular and canonical: 'a process whereby texts are produced, exchanged, and used' that is part of a larger 'continuous sociohistoric process in which persons, artifacts, practices, institutions, and communities are being formed and reformed'.[5] In other words, in addition to providing access to born-digital primary sources, text mining the Internet would also digital humanists to study literate activities like reception, knowledge formation, and cultural transmission on an unprecedented scale. Harnessing web data can also afford increased opportunities for public engagement in humanities-driven research. The recent attention that Benjamin Schmidt's 'Gendered Language in Teacher Reviews' picked up in the popular press, for example, highlights how a tool designed for the study of nineteenth century archives can be applied to data retrieved from the Internet to promote publically the values and goals of humanities scholarship.[6]

Despite the promise of the Internet as a source for humanities data, one of the most powerful techniques for retrieving data, 'web scraping', currently occupies a liminal space. Briefly, web scraping is the use of software to automatically navigate web pages and retrieve information from them. As will be discussed below, web scraping software does not follow the expected browsing behavior of a human reader, leading legal critics to argue that it is a form of intellectual property theft and damaging to technological infrastructure. Many of these attitudes are due to the fact that web scraping is used primarily towards commercial ends. Yet projects like The Internet Archive harvest data explicitly for the purpose of supporting open-ended, non-commercial research.[7] The Internet is therefore a complex data source not only due to its scale and the wide range of writing practices taking place across it, but also due to the steps that academic researchers must take to distinguish themselves from commercial and malicious web scraping in order to protect themselves from legal action and avoid inadvertently damaging the websites they pull data from. Following some basic definitions of Internet data retrieval techniques, this essay explores how digital humanists are better positioned than we may imagine to manage the Internet's complexities, examines the ethic and legal dimensions of web scraping, and concludes with a short description of resources for scholars new to Internet data retrieval.

2. WHAT IS WEB SCRAPING?

Web scraping is a term encompassing a variety of data retrieval and extraction techniques that scan, identify, and capture information from human-readable webpages. In this context, a data source can be anything from a minimally structured file repository, a static webpage composed in HyperText Markup Language (HTML), or complex documents generated dynamically by a web server, such as the comments section to a newspaper article. While there are a number of common tools found across a variety of web scraping projects, there are no one-size-fits-all programs available due to the wide variety of content hosting platforms and the pace at which both they and web language standards change. Yet well-aggregated data is an important component of Internet commerce, and as a result web scraping has become a highly lucrative tool for companies that provide search engines, pricing information, and advertising services. While large companies like Google dedicate staff to maintaining and improving their own web scraping software, tools available to the public are often marketed by their designers as part of an economic and consumer research service rather than as stand-alone software applications.

Although the two share some of the same techniques and challenges, web archiving and web scraping are two distinct practices. There are a growing number of non-profit institutions, university-led projects, and government data services currently working to archive web sources for the purpose of open-ended research including The Internet Archive, PANDORA, and the Internet Memory

Foundation.[8] Unlike web archiving, which seeks to reproduce the source in its complete original context and form, web scraping is typically targeted towards retrieving only specific types of data. Although web scraping projects will likely involve an archival step, the resulting archives typically consist only of materials relevant to the project's analytic procedures. For example, a project working with images may initially capture textual data in order to use it to identify the location of image files whereas a text-driven project would ignore image references entirely, and both would ignore the Cascading Style Sheets files used to lay out web components in the browser window. Web archiving projects, however, can be a valuable resource for web scraping research, especially since they are likely the only way to access websites that are no longer live, have deleted content, or have otherwise undergone significant changes.

Non-malicious Internet data retrieval can be divided roughly into two categories: formally supported and informally permitted. Formally supported data retrieval differs from web scraping in that is performed through an Application Programming Interface (API) or other framework implemented explicitly to handle and respond to automated data requests. In practice, these frameworks often operate through commands appended to the end of a URL, returning a tightly structured bundle of data rather than an HTML document. Websites that permit API access typically provide documentation detailing how commands can be combined to execute particular types of searches. This documentation will usually outline any explicit restrictions on data retrieval or use. Websites may require API users to register accounts in order to maintain the same data protection or privacy standards that web browser users are subject to, as is the case with social media sites that provide API access like Twitter or Facebook, or impose size limits on data retrieval in order to prevent a small number of API users from monopolising bandwidth.

In contrast to formally supported retrieval, web scraping targets sources where retrieval is informally permitted in the sense that a website neither explicitly supports nor forbids automated data retrieval. Web scraping is sometimes colloquially referred as 'screen scraping' because most techniques involve downloading the same documents used to render webpages on-screen for human consumption and filtering through their HTML code for specific types of information. Web scraping is, in this sense, similar to other forms of unstructured text mining because it requires researchers to closely examine archetypical documents in a collection and develop a heuristic that can filter out irrelevant data. Web scraping algorithms are thus often tailored to specific websites. Even if two websites are both hosted on Wordpress platforms, for example, they may be configured differently and not share the same page addressing scheme, tag definitions, or page layout structures. While web scraping requires more upfront planning than working through an API, it nonetheless opens up larger portions of the Internet to data extraction. Many digital humanities archival projects, such as

ACTUP Oral History Project,[9] the Influenza Encyclopedia,[10] or the September 11 Digital Archive,[11] lack API access but do not forbid data retrieval. While web scraping could allow us to incorporate the primary sources that these and others projects curate into projects involving large-scale text analysis, there are a number of methodological and ethical concerns that researchers must first consider.

3. COMPLEX METHODOLOGIES

While Internet research is already a well-established field, the humanities are vastly underrepresented within it.[12] Among those humanists studying cultural activity on the Internet, there is little research that addresses the complexities of scale that the Internet as a research context introduces. New media studies has up to this point largely reproduced methodologies found in literary criticism,[13] ethnography,[14] discourse analysis,[15] and visual cultural studies.[16] Projects like these have made important, foundational contributions to new media studies because they highlight the unique cultural work that digital media perform on top of or in place of the older forms they remediate.[17] They also succeed in drawing in the critical, interpretive, and cultural theory that drives humanities scholarship into areas of our society that are often heavily dominated by a technical rhetoric that displaces all other perspectives. Internet research could benefit from the humanities' critical reflectivity, a perspective that has led studies like those cited above to question the technologically-driven assumptions about the role the Internet plays in our cultural history as well as the broader sociopolitical consequences of our increasing dependence on it. Yet humanities research on Internet culture has remained largely committed to the tradition of the close reading of primary sources and so has not taken advantage of the scale that web scraping could afford. If we choose to take advantage of the scale that automated retrieval and analysis of web data affords, then it is critically important that we consider the new challenges that the Internet's intertextual complexity introduces.

Even though scholarship on hypertext theory tends to focus on electronic literature, many studies highlights the structural differences between physical and digital documents, making it a useful starting point for considering the Internet as a complex data source.[18] By definition, hypertexts exist as an assemblage of component documents that are linked together by intertextual references that readers can chose to follow to instantaneously shift their awareness to different locations within the assemblage. As George P. Landow argues, humanists are already implicitly familiar with hypertextual forms because our research and writing practices emphasise the tracing, interpreting, and synthesising of intertextual networks. But hypertexts take intertextuality a step further than physical documents by encouraging a de-centered, multi-directional form of literate activity. According to Landow, if the goal of scholarly writing has traditionally been to arrange disparate sources into a well-formed argument, then the intertextuality of physical documents resembles a straight line that branches off to other documents. Hypertexts would by comparison resemble a rhizome, offering no singular point of entry or navigational strategy, requiring readers to develop and continually revise their reading strategies.[19] Hypertext theory thus raises at least two concerns that humanities web scraping must address: how to account for the complex construction of hypertexts in an automated retrieval or extraction work flow, and how to leverage that complexity to aid analysis. Even a single website can be a complex network of digital objects that includes images, textual passages, interactive buttons, video, or hyperlinks, each defined distinctly in HTML. A single reader's literate activity rarely takes place at a single location, instead unfolding over several websites in a variety of genres such as social media, blogging, link aggregation sites, specialised forums, online periodicals, and the comments sections that open up a space for interaction on all of them.

Humanists, in short, need a methodological vocabulary or hypertextual taxonomy that allows us to identify readily the specific components within these assemblages that are most germane to our research questions as well as to articulate clearly practices for locating, retrieving, and analyzing those components using automated tools at scale. In arguing for the need for an Internet historiography, Niels Brügger lays the groundwork for such a taxonomy with his model of 'web strata' (see Table 1).[20] Brügger proposes five terms—web element, web page, web site, web sphere, and web as a whole—that together represent a spectrum of abstraction that allows researchers to specify whether they are observing phenomena from the level of basic technical components to whole systems. Beyond providing a working vocabulary, Brügger's proposal of 'web sphere' is defined in a way that allows us to establish broad community contexts that are not reliant on national categories, as humanities disciplines like literature and history often are. Despite Brügger's caution to readers that these strata can be nested within one another, his model lacks a clear way to describe hybrid components produced through nesting. Blog comments are here a useful example because they are more complex than elements but not complex enough to be considered pages. At the level of HTML code, comments are often comprised of one or more static text fields, text entry forms, and sometimes a profile avatar image, all bundled together between ' < div > ' tags and often dynamically generated through interactions with a backend database. Treated as a whole, comments exist in a space somewhere between elements and pages. At least superficially, bundling elements together to form a component with a singular function resembles the object-oriented programming practice of creating abstract components out of basic ones. Adding a sixth strata, the 'web object', thus updates Brügger's taxonomy to account for web element

Table 1. Brügger's Web Strata (Modified).

Strata	Definition	Example(s)
Web Element	The most basic components of the web, considered either from the user's perspective or in the encoded markup languages used by browsers to render the web	Images, text, tables, buttons, hyperlinks, and their representations in HTML/CSS
Web Object*	A combination of web elements nested in a container element that functions as a single component of a larger document	Comment box, tweet, submission form, browser-based game, JavaScript app, news feed
Web Page	A collection of web elements and/or objects presented to users as a complete document	Blog entry, journal article, Wikipedia entry
Web Site	A collection of web pages representing an online publication, resource, community, organisation, company, university, or data repository	adho.org, theguardian.com, illinois.edu, fsf.org, data.gov
Web Sphere	Web activity related to an abstract theme or event that spans multiple sites and/or genres of literate activity	Social media, blogging, memes, viral videos, online journalism, political campaigns, online activism
Web as a Whole	Concepts that 'transcend' the web itself, including the technological infrastructure that supports the web	Digital media theory, histories of the Internet, new media ecology, web programming languages, Internet protocols (TCP/IP)

*Information from this row does not appear in Brügger's essay

nesting. With this taxonomy in mind, this section closes by examining two digital humanities projects that address challenges of data complexity that are structurally similar to those that academic web scraping projects will face.

Although there are many large-scale text analytics projects currently under way in the digital humanities, Ted Underwood's 'Understanding Genre in a Collection of a Million Volumes' uses a taxonomy that bears striking similarities to Brügger's.[21] Underwood's original premise was to study genre, a term normally used to categorise to whole documents. Underwood's data set consists of over 800,000 scanned books and periodicals from HathiTrust—a partnership between more than 100 libraries that hosts approximately 13.8 million digitised documents—in the form of bundles of scanned pages. Because his previous experiments on a smaller, hand-picked collection of books structured as whole documents had shown promising results, he initially established the 'volume' as his basic unit of analysis. His first trials therefore used a collation preparation step that joined the pages of each book or periodical into whole volumes.[22] During his initial trials, he determined that his machine learning algorithms struggled to distinguish between volume-level genres that human readers could easily discern. To address this problem, he decided to complicate his data set by adding a stratum called 'section' between page and volume. This step would allow him to train models capable of identifying more finely grained genres that were nested within volumes and construct volume-level classifications by examining sequences of section types.[23] Underwood's project thus leverages the complex relationships within an assemblage of textual components at various levels of his taxonomy, redefining the data structures of his collection in a way that allows him to translate the abstract cultural questions driving his research into algorithmic analysis. For humanities web scraping, the lesson here is that a hypertextual taxonomy not only allows us to more precisely delineate our research questions, but also to create data structures and relationships between web components that can help us negotiate between our disciplinary goals and the complex challenges introduced by conducting Internet research at scale.

Despite this valuable lesson, Underwood's project is still very much concerned with mapping the assemblages he creates back onto traditional literary taxonomies. The 'Viral Texts: Mapping Networks of Reprinting in Nineteenth Century Newspapers and Magazines' project, on the other hand, serves as an example of how to address intertextuality on a scale and at a complexity that approximates the challenge of asking questions at the level of web spheres. As Ryan Cordell notes, nineteenth century newspapers were replete with republished snippets, often without attribution: 'the value of widely reprinted snippets derived from their movement through the exchange system' rather than 'the genius of individual creators.'[24] For the most part, the value of these snippets was lost during their textual transmission, and scholarship on nineteenth century culture has 'remained largely bound up with exemplary authors: Fern, Lippard, Yonge, or Hawthorne, Poe, even Dickens.'[25] The project's goal, in short, is to abandon the traditional forms of authority associated with identity and instead explore an authority defined through reference. The project thus resonates strongly with past scholarship on hypertextual intertextuality. Cordell and his team used five token n-grams, or unique phrases of five words in length, to identify reprinted snippets, producing a record of intertextual references that are functionally similar to the hyperlinks of web pages. Using this record, they are able to trace both the geographic spread of reprints but also which genres were being reprinted, effectively mapping spheres of circulation. As Cordell concludes, their findings 'trouble accounts of antebellum print culture that cohere primarily around literary genres such as fiction and poetry' by showing that 'useful knowledge' and other informational content were much more commonly reprinted.[26] Following a similar methodology, and benefiting from the explicit referencing of hyperlinks, digital humanists could ask broad questions about the literate activity unfolding over the web, especially because using the Internet as a data source would afford access to text written by both professionals and amateurs, a distinction that is often not available when working with more formal archives. Shifting our attention to content related to specific events would allow us to see how the public understands key theoretical issues important to the humanities such as evident in their responses to events in the media, television shows, movies, or contemporary literature, on topics such as gender, race, sexuality, or our relationship to postcolonial states, among others.

4. EVALUATING THE LEGALITY AND ETHICS OF WEB SCRAPING FOR ACADEMIC RESEARCH

Despite its increasing prevalence, the legal status and ethical dimensions of web scraping are still being debated. Malicious data retrieval that exploits security flaws or exposes password-protected data can be subject to broad cybersecurity laws like the United States' Computer Fraud and Abuse Act[27] or one of the European Union's several directives pertaining to information security.[28] While there is some agreement among legal rulings intentionally that web scraping does not inherently violate intellectual property laws, recent cases in both the United States' and European Union's courts consider whether the practice damages the value of data or inflicts economic harm on data hosts.[29] As with many of the technological practices and frameworks that digital humanists engage with, much of the web scraping taking place today over the Internet occurs as part of commercial activity, and as a result many of the attitudes, opinions, and rulings, surrounding the practice were not formed with academic research in mind. It is therefore vitally important that humanists intervene in these discussions by establishing research guidelines, much like academics working in human subject research have already done, that allow policy makers and Internet technologists to distinguish their research from work being done by price aggregators, search engine providers, marketing departments, and search engine optimisers.

Generally speaking, web scraping is considered legally permissible so long as it does not intentionally interfere with a data source's commercial activities or try to misrepresent the ownership of reproducible content. Because copyright law in most Western countries could potentially apply to almost all content on the web, the legality of web scraping copyrighted content is therefore often determined by the purpose of retrieval.[30] Merely reproducing retrieved data, for example, may be considered a violation of copyright; however, most text analysis algorithms transform and reduce documents significantly. Sharing the results of an analysis, especially if it explicitly references or otherwise directs readers back to the original source of that data, could be considered permissible provided it does not reduce the original data's commercial value or harm the data's creator. While the applicability of copyright is easy to assess on documents, it can be harder to determine when applied to information retrieved from databases. Although United States copyright law does not cover 'factual data'—the contents of a databases such as timetables, titles, names, viewer counts, or even survey responses—it can protect components of a database produced through a creative process—such as database schema, visualisations, and any questions or surveys used to generate data.[31] Unlike the United States, the European Union's Database Directive explicitly protects against certain forms of factual data retrieval without the need to demonstrate a creative dimension; however, at the same time the directive also allows for non-commercial research. One key legal advantage that humanities projects have in this regard is the largely non-commercial nature of their research, which is often practiced within a tradition of preserving and respecting original sources.

In addition to examining the intent of web scraping, courts have also begun to consider whether the practice can be done without harming technological infrastructure. Because web scraping algorithms are capable of accessing web pages much faster than human readers, they can have a detrimental effect on the machines hosting a website by overloading them with requests—causing a server crash—or inadvertently locking other visitors out of a website by using all of a host's bandwidth. Whereas earlier cases argued that all web scraping was potentially harmful to data hosts, more recent cases have been decided in favor of web scrapers that demonstrate an ethical awareness by acknowledging, accounting for, and minimising the risk of potential damage that mass retrieval can cause to a data source's computer systems and network infrastructure.[32] The voluntary ethical guidelines mentioned in these rulings are defined in the 'robots exclusion protocol.' First proposed in 1994 by Martijn Koster, the robots exclusion protocol uses a simple text file called 'robots.txt' located in the root directory of a website to specify locations on a website that automated tools should ignore. Each entry in a robots.txt file consists of two or more lines of code: an initial line identifying a 'user-agent', or the identification string that all software includes when making a retrieval request, that is followed by one or more lines identifying which directories software with matching user-agent strings should not search. Unfortunately, the robots exclusion protocol does not include any way for data sources to request that web scrapers limit the rate of their requests. Although there is no de facto standard rate limit, scholars should use their best judgment and follow any voluntary limits stated in a website's terms of use. For an overview of how to determine whether a website imposes restrictions on web scraping or may view the practice as malicious, see Table 2.

Although the robots exclusion protocol is an excellent starting point, following its voluntary restrictions alone will not sufficiently distinguish digital humanists from commercial web scrapers. In addition to respecting the access restrictions defined by site owners, academic researchers should also take

Table 2. Overview of Internet Data Retrieval Ethics by Access Type.

Access Type	Retrieval Type	Definition	Recommendation
Hard Open	Explicitly supported	Explicitly allows for automated search and retrieval by including a data API to facilitate access	Follow any guidelines and restrictions described in the API's documentation pages
Soft Open	Informally permitted	Does not include a data API but could support screen scraping. No page on the site explicitly states that web scraping is forbidden	Look for robots.txt and follow and guidelines defined therein. If no robots.txt is provided, follow your best judgment about which parts of the site should be excluded. Use a safe retrieval request rate.
Soft Closed	Potentially malicious	Does not password protect content or specify clear restrictions in robots.txt but explicitly states on a 'terms of use' page that web scraping is forbidden or restricted	The site owner may not have considered academic research when developing a web scraping policy. Contact the owner and ask for permission. Alternatively, check for copies of the website in a web archiving project that supports automated retrieval like the Internet Archive.
Hard Closed	Potentially malicious	Content is password protected or subject to some other security check	Exclude from project. Some services that host password protected data, like JSTOR, may be willing to make it available to researchers through a security agreement.

steps to identify themselves and the purpose of their web scraping. Because most web servers keep logs of user-agent requests, humanities researchers should write tools with user-agent strings that include their name and the address to a web page that explains the goals of their research, details their web scraping procedures, and provides contact information for feedback about their procedures or for requests to be excluded from the project. These pages would serve a similar propose to the informed consent forms required by most university ethics review boards. Descriptions of web scraping procedures should not only outline the web crawling strategy, but specify what data is being retrieved, the frequency that retrieval requests are made, and how long data will be kept. While commercial web scrapers often choose to keep their techniques secret, digital humanists should make every effort to make their methods as transparent as possible. These additional steps are not only in line with ethical guidelines followed by academics in fields that are subject to ethics review but will also assist those new to web scraping in locating example work flows.

5. BASIC SKILLS AND RESOURCES

As noted above, there are already good examples of text analysis in the digital humanities that will share much in common with Internet-focused research projects. Fortunately, the primary differences between web scraping and other forms of text analysis are in the retrieval and extraction steps that precede analysis. Like large text mining projects already underway in the digital humanities, web scraping will require individual researchers or project teams to organise large corpora as well as generate and manage metadata for their collections. As an initial first step, digital humanists can begin web scraping by adapting their existing preprocessing steps to handle documents written in a mark-up language. Once data has been retrieved from the Internet, digital humanists can extract textual data and store it in a form for use with tools already familiar to researchers in the field like WordSmith, MALLET, Gephi, or Bookworm.

For those without much experience with text mining, the Voyant Tools project is an excellent source to learn about the kinds of data that humanists can extract from Internet sources because it already supports text extraction from webpages.[33] Because HTML documents typically include other media types in addition to text and because even text elements are combined into more complex objects, online demonstration tools that commercial web scraping services use for advertising purposes can work well as learning tools to illustrate the assemblage structure of web pages. Unfortunately, online, user-friendly tools are limited in their ability to capture data because the modern World Wide Web is a mixture of constantly changing standards. Humanists interested in web scraping should therefore have a working knowledge of HTML in order to identify the mark-up tags that frame elements or objects they are interested in studying. To assist in identification, most modern web browsers now include a readily usable 'Developer View' or 'Inspector' tool that displays the HTML for an open page and highlights lines defining any elements or objects that users mouse over.

Despite the limitations of user-friendly web scraping tools, there are a number of powerful and highly customised programming libraries that can help digital humanists handle both the retrieval and extraction of web data. Many programming languages now include standard XML parsing libraries that can be used to quickly navigate and extract information from an HTML document, but more specialised libraries like BeautifulSoup for Python[34] or Nokogiri for Ruby[35] also exist that offer better support for navigating complex web pages. While an HTML parsing library can be enough to manage smaller web scraping projects, webcrawler libraries like Scrapy[36] or Apache Nutch[37] can not only assist with batch retrieval but also with the organisation and management of an archived web sphere.

6. CONCLUSION

Web scraping not only offers scholars of twentieth and twenty-first century culture a chance to contribute to the digital humanities but also a chance to ensure that the interests of the humanities are represented in Internet Studies as well as in the growing discussions around big data. For new media studies and Internet history, web scraping offers scholars a chance to ask new questions that were not possible, or very difficult, to explore previously due to the sheer number of archived websites in data repositories like the Internet Archive. With more new media genres being invented every year, treating the Internet as a complex data source could also potentially open up new fields of study or contribute to new forms of creative expression.

While the World Wide Web as a complex data source offers new methodological challenges for digital humanities, these challenges are not without precedent. As this essay has shown, there are already projects in the digital humanities addressing problems similar to those that web scraping projects will face and ethical traditions that can serve as models for engaging with data hosts. This essay has highlighted those projects to sketch out many of the initial hurdles humanities web scraping will face; however, these similarities also suggest that the lessons learned from the development of web scraping techniques can contribute back to projects working with digitised, print materials.

END NOTES

[1] M. L. Sample, 'Unseen and Unremarked On: Don DeLillo and the Failure of the Digital Humanities', in *Debates in the Digital Humanities*, ed. M. K. Gold (Minneapolis, 2012): 187–201; M. Jockers, 'Orphans', in *Macroanalysis* (Urbana, 2013): 171–6.

[2] Of the more than 100 institutions listed on the HathiTrust's partnerships page, for example, only two are located outside of North America and only one from a country where English isn't the primary language. This information was retrieved from the HathiTrust's Community page, https:// www.hathitrust.org/community, last accessed on 31 July, 2015.

[3] H. Jenkins, 'The Cultural Logic of Media Convergence', *International Journal of Cultural Studies* 7 (2004): 33–43.

[4] M. Condis, 'No homosexuals in *Star Wars*? BioWare, "gamer" identity, and the politics of privilege in a convergence culture', *Convergence* 21 (2015): 198–212; M. Verboord, 'The impact of peer-produced criticism on cultural evaluation: A multilevel analysis of discourse employment in online and offline film reviews', *New Media and Society* 16 (2014): 921–40.

[5] P. Prior, *Writing/Disciplinarity: A Sociohistoric Account of Literary Activity in the Academy* (New York, 1998): 139.

[6] B. Schmidt, *Gendered Language in Teaching Reviews*, http://benschmidt.org/profGender, last accessed 31 July, 2015.

[7] *Internet Archive Terms of Use*, https://archive.org/about/terms.php, last accessed 5 November, 2015.

[8] *The Internet Archive*, http://www.archive.org, last accessed 31 July, 2015; *PANDORA: Australia's Web Archive*, http://pandora.nla.gov.au, last accessed 31 July, 2015; The Internet Memory Foundation, *Archive The Net*, http://archivethe.net/en, last accessed 31 July, 2015.

[9] *ACTUP Oral History Project*, http://www.actuporalhistory.org/index1.html, last accessed 31 July, 2015.

[10] *The American Influenza Episode of 1918: A Digital Encyclopedia*, http://www.influenzaarchive.org, last accessed 31 July, 2015.

[11] *The September 11 Digital Archive*, http://911digitalarchive.org, last accessed 31 July, 2015.

[12] This would include both traditional forms of research that use the Internet as a venue (i.e., to host surveys or access digitised versions of print texts) as well as research on the Internet itself. Whereas the former has quietly become part of standard research practice, the latter is growing into an interdisciplinary field. Yet most of the publications linked to on the Association for Internet Research's website are authored by scholars working in social science and computer science fields. Among those from Communications departments, methods vary between humanities and social science traditions. For more information, see: http://aoir.org/publications/

[13] I. Bogost, *Unit Operations: An Approach to Video Game Criticism* (Cambridge, 2006)

[14] T. Boellstorff, *Coming of Age in Second Life: An Anthropologist Explores the Virtually Human* (Princeton, 2008); M. Gray, *Out in the Country: Youth, Media, and Queer Visibility in Rural America* (New York, 2009).

[15] R. Black, *Adolescents and Online Fan Fiction* (New York, 2008).

[16] L. Nakamura, *Digitizing Race: Visual Cultures of the Internet* (Minneapolis, 2008).

[17] For an overview of foundational concepts see: J. Bolter and R. Grusin, *Remediation: Understanding New Media* (Cambridge, 2000); L. Manovich, *The Language of New Media* (Cambridge, 2002).

[18] J. Bolter, *Writing Space: The Computer, Hypertext, and the History of Writing* (Hillsdale, 1991); E. Aarseth, *Cybertext: Perspectives on Ergodic Literature* (Baltimore, 1997); J. Murray, *Hamlet on the Holodeck: The Future of Narrative in Cyberspace* (New York, 1997); S. Gaggi, *From Text to Hypertext: Decentering the Subject in Fiction, Film, the Visual, and Electronic Media* (Philadelphia, 1998); J. McGann, *Radiant Textuality: Literature After the World Wide Web* (New York, 2004).

[19] *Hypertext 3.0: Critical Theory and New Media in an Era of Globalization* (Baltimore, 2006).

[20] Table 1 is derived from N. Brügger, 'Web historiography and Internet Studies: Challenges and perspectives', *New Media Studies*, 15 (2012), 752–64.

[21] Underwood's thought process is well documented on his blog. This paragraph is largely a summary of the project with references to only a select few entries or related articles. For more details, see: http://tedunderwood.com/

22 T. Underwood and J. Sellers, 'The Emergence of Literary Diction', *Journal of the Digital* Humanities 2 (2012), http://journalofdigitalhumanities.org/1-2/the-emergence-of-literary-diction-by-ted-underwood-and-jordan-sellers, last accessed 31 July, 2015.

23 T. Underwood, M. Black, L. Auvil, and B. Capitanu, 'Mapping Mutable Genres in Structurally Complex Volumes', *Proceedings of the 2013 IEEE International Conference on Big Data* (Santa Clara, 2013).

24 R. Cordell, 'Reprinting, Circulation, and the Network Author in Antebellum Newspapers', http://ryancordell.org/research/reprinting-circulation-and-the-network-author-in-antebellum-newspapers, last accessed 31 July, 2015.

25 R. Cordell, 'Reprinting, Circulation, and the Network Author'

26 R. Cordell, 'Reprinting, Circulation, and the Network Author'

27 Because *Craigslist v. 3Taps* (N.N. Cal. 16 August 2013); *USA v. Swartz* (1:11-cr-10260)

28 For example, Directive 2013/40 'on attacks against information systems', http://eur-lex.europa.eu/LexUriServ/LexUriServ.do?uri=OJ:L:2013:218:0008:0014:EN:HTML, last accessed 12 November, 2015, or Directive 96/6/E 'on the legal protection of databases', http://eur-lex.europa.eu/LexUriServ/LexUriServ.do?uri=CELEX:31996L0009:EN:HTML, last accessed 12 November, 2015.

29 *QVC, Inc. v Resulty, LLC* (S.D.P.A Mar. 13, 2015); *Ryanair Ltd v PR Aviation BV* (C-30/14)

30 For an example of a recent case centering on the validity of reproducing news items on an aggregation website, see *Associated Press v. Meltwater U.S. Holdings, Inc.* (S.D.N.Y. Mar. 21, 2013). Popular aggregators like Google News avoid the problems Meltwater faced by 'transforming' the news stories through clustering and providing explicit links to their original web sources.

31 U.S. Copyright Office, *Report on Legal Protection for Databases*, http://www.copyright.gov/reports/dbase.html, last accessed 31 July, 2015.

32 In *American Airlines, Inc. v Farechase, Inc.* (67 T.X. Mar. 8, 2003), American won an injunction halting Farechase's web scraping by arguing that their aggregation of airline ticket prices was potentially hurting their business. The case was settled out of court before a judicial opinion could be authored. More recently in *QVC, Inc. v Resulty, LLC* (S.D.P.A Mar. 13, 2015), the courts suggested that web scraping was not harmful provided the algorithms used explicitly identified themselves as non-human and respected any limitations on access requested by the data source.

33 *Voyant Tools: Reveal Your Text*, http://voyeurtools.org, last accessed 31 July, 2015.

34 *Beautiful Soup*, http://www.crummy.com/software/BeautifulSoup, last accessed 31 July, 2015.

35 *Nokogiri*, http://www.nokogiri.org, last accessed 31 July, 2015.

36 *Scrapy*, http://scrapy.org, last accessed 31 July, 2015.

37 *Apache Nutch*, http://nutch.apache.org, last accessed 31 July, 2015.

MECHANIZED MARGIN TO DIGITIZED CENTER: BLACK FEMINISM'S CONTRIBUTIONS TO COMBATTING ERASURE WITHIN THE DIGITAL HUMANITIES

NICOLE M. BROWN, RUBY MENDENHALL, MICHAEL L. BLACK, MARK VAN MOER, ASSATA ZERAI AND KAREN FLYNN

Abstract   *Computational analysis and digital humanities are far from neutral processes and sites unimpeded by the political, social and economic context in which they emerged and are utilized. As an interdisciplinary field, the digital humanities have transformed the relationship of humans to computers broadly conceived. At the same time, the methods, theories, perspectives and the concomitant digital tools developed are being criticized for reproducing the social divisions that exist in society. The effort to recover Black women's subjectivities from the digital minefield is not without its challenges, reflected in our study which searched approximately 800,000 books, newspapers, and articles in the HathiTrust and JSTOR Digital Libraries. The goal was to identify perceptions and lived experiences of Black women that emerged and the resulting knowledge that developed. The project team discovered multiple challenges related to the rescue and recovery of Black women's standpoints or group knowledge. This essay explores how even as computational analysis has embedded biases, it can be utilized to recover the experiences of Black women from within the digitized record. Thus, computational analysis and all that it encompasses not only makes visible Black women's experiences, but also expands the scope of the digital humanities.*

Keywords: computational analysis, black women's live, feminist studies, corpora analysis, bias

International Journal of Humanities and Arts Computing 10.1 (2016): 110–125
DOI: 10.3366/ijhac.2016.0163
© Edinburgh University Press 2016
www.euppublishing.com/journal/ijhac

INTRODUCTION

As an interdisciplinary field, the digital humanities, while having transformed the relationship of humans to computers broadly conceived[1], are also open to criticism for the use of methods, theories, perspectives, and concomitant digital tools which reproduce the social divisions that exist in a male-dominated technocratic American society. While U.S. based digital humanities scholars continue to stretch the limits of computational analysis' application to digitized text, we remain hesitant to use the same technological advances to better understand issues related to identity and power (as conceived in the U.S.). More specifically, an examination of how identities are shaped and reshaped by vectors of race, gender, class and sexuality, are relational resulting in hierarchical power relations, which are intricately connected to the production of knowledge. Indeed, new opportunities for the digital humanities rest in the possibilities available to explore many of these issues and to chart a new course for the discipline by featuring previously marginalized voices and perspectives. Yet, the problem with such an uncritical approach where we adopt digital humanities technologies wholesale is that, in many cases, it can serve to reify the very power dynamics, which limit the field in its endeavors toward expanding useful knowledge. This essay is certainly not the first to make such a claim. Recent and forthcoming essays by Tara McPherson, Angel David Nieves, Marla Jaksch, and Martha Nell Smith have challenged the unacknowledged racial, ethnic, and gendered assumptions underlying digital archiving and software tools.[2] However, the increasing visibility of large scale text analysis projects has often been accompanied by a problematic, implicit assumption that large digital archives afford a more complete or objective view of cultural history. While some scholars working in this field, and especially Ted Underwood, have acknowledged and expressed discomfort over the perception that their work is somehow providing a more objective or complete perspective, there is comparatively little available research in large-scale text analysis that addresses writing by women and people of color. Computational analysis and digital humanities are thus far from neutral processes and sites unimpeded by the political, social and economic context in which they emerged and are utilized. As a result, the purpose of this essay is to disrupt the current ways in which computational analysis is used and to expose how these processes have embedded biases which can be addressed through the intervention of U.S. based Black feminism.[3] Using lessons and insight gained from the project team's participation in a ground-breaking 'Black Women Big Data' project, the authors structurally mimic tenets of Black feminism within (as many as possible of) the steps of computational analysis. Black feminism combines methods and theory to dismantle privilege and reification processes, which normally construct (mechanized) socio-political margins. From corpora creation through the process of analysis, Black feminism offers interventions that serve to dismantle embedded privilege and reification and (digitally) center the experiences of Black women within digital humanities research. We argue in this essay that computational analysis can be used in a deliberate effort to combat the erasure of Black women's experiences, and to uncover the gaps in themes that prevent researchers from obtaining more complete embodiments of Black women's lived experiences.

The goal of the 'Black Women Big Data' study involved searching approximately 800,000 books, newspapers, and articles in the HathiTrust and JSTOR Digital Libraries[4] to identify Black American women's perceptions about U.S. social structures and their lived experiences. During the study, the research team discovered multiple challenges related to the rescue and recovery of Black women's standpoints. These databases are two of the largest available resources for digitized print material, holding over several millions of documents each; however, both are housed and administered in the United States and comprised largely of English language resources. Because this study focused on Black American sources and experiences, these limitations were acceptable. Regardless of its incarnation, internationally, Black feminist theorizing shares some similarities with its U.S. counterpart. The study applied topic modeling to documents from both databases to identify what types of conversations appeared in various genres of text (African American Studies, poetry, policy, psychology, sociology, etc.) and data visualizations to identify spikes in certain topics during specific historical periods. In this essay we share our learnings from the original study and argue the importance of distinguishing between formal and informal sources of data and understanding the political aspects of knowledge creation. Recognizing these structural realities allows researchers to uncover and address the limitations and power dynamics of knowledge creation about the lived experiences of Black women (epistemology) that are embedded within the computational analysis process. This uncovering occurs with a critical read of computational analysis through the lens of Black feminist theory. In centering Black women's voices and experiences, the researchers interrogate current knowledge sources and methods and reimagine new uses for digital humanities, which validate and incorporate Black feminist ways of knowing.

COLORBLIND LOGIC: BIG DATA AS APOLITICAL AND OBJECTIVE

Because many of the English language digital humanities text analysis projects locate themselves within the American and British literary canons, even when incorporating 'the great unread', there remains an implicit embedded privileging of whiteness surrounding the theorization and application of computational methods.[5] This uncritical lens is a result of institutional forces in the matrix of domination that creates multiplicative advantages for specific racialized, gendered and classed bodies, specifically White heterosexual males.[6] At the same time, however, scholars like Adeline Koh and Tara McPherson have observed that the digital humanities often overlooks questions about women and people of color entirely.[7] Dorothy Kim and Jesse Stommel have also argued for the value of disruptions within the digital humanities.[8] Black feminism not only challenges the embedded whiteness and maleness of computational analysis but goes further to consider the intersectional aspects of identity markers such as race, class, gender and sexuality and how these interconnected identities impact research. The complex politics of race, class, gender, and sexuality can already be difficult to represent in non-digital scholarship. Trying to represent them algorithmically may be even more difficult, especially since many within the digital humanities are already skeptical of the capacity for 'distant reading' to represent the essential, nuanced experience of context that is often key to addressing questions involving these subjects.

Finding ways to incorporate computational analysis into research on race, class, gender, and sexuality would thus serve to decolonize the digital humanities from its aversion to addressing issues of identity and power distribution.[9] Expanding the scope of Black feminist epistemological approaches to include text mining techniques expands our ways of knowing and relating to these methods, exposing the subjectivity of computational analysis and opening up spaces that can empower and amplify the voices/narratives of the marginalized. This article, in short, argues that the digital humanities does not have to be an 'escape' from theory but rather can be a way to explore theoretical questions that are difficult to address due to the limitations of human labor. These limitations are most commonly expressed through issues of power relations via digital humanities tools.[10] These tools are not a way to replace or supplant the intellectual work of the scholar but rather a way to supplement the labor of managing an archive that precedes the critical analysis.

WHAT BLACK FEMINIST THEORY TELLS US ABOUT KNOWLEDGE CREATION, PRODUCTION AND LEGITIMACY

Epistemology is the study of knowledge, its nature, validity, and limits. Collins asserts that epistemology is the 'standards used to assess what we know or why we believe what we believe'.[11] When considering the study of knowledge and standards, Black women outside of the academy are often not seen as knowledge creators or part of the Black women's intellectual tradition. In addition, the knowledge produced by Black women academics are often viewed as illegitimate by some mainstream scholars due to issues of objectivity and the combination of theory and praxis.[12] When taking a Black feminist approach to epistemology, both of these erasures are reclaimed.

113

Incorporating the tenets of Black feminist thought during data collection, analysis, and writing provides insight about how to study Black women's lives, culture and history and how to ensure that their experiences are rescued, recovered, centered and preserved. Black feminist thought demands an attention to race, class, gender (and other) intersectionality. Zerai describes features of intersectionality as:

> Multiplicative analysis, recognizing that there is no singular experience of being a woman; analyzing multiple dimensions, including race, class, gender, sexuality, nation, and other spheres of inequality; acknowledging the simultaneity of oppressions; considering the importance of context, examining phenomena by including contextual as well as individual factors; analyzing resistance; and examining relationality in variant experiences of groups based on members' relative social locations.[13]

This relational approach to understanding intersecting social locations and their impact on Black women's lived experiences allows for a deeper, contextual analysis which serves to recognize the embedded multiplicity of knowledge creation. Knowledge production and legitimization processes expose embedded power dynamics between individuals, systems, and institutions in that they highlight who grants authority to create knowledge deemed worthy of acknowledgement and study.[14] Data and its sources are legitimized by those with authority to determine what is 'important', and what is deemed important is subjective based on the legitimizing institution's positionality and agenda. Oppressive systems and institutions are often reified as marginalized groups are further de-legitimized, viewed in few cases as a site of study, and rarely as a source from which legitimized knowledge may be obtained. The very institutionalization of knowledge production embeds biases that insist knowledge looks and sounds a certain way, and those whose lives and voices are marginalized rarely, if ever, determine or achieve such standards. Black feminism acknowledges marginalized narratives, specifically those narratives of Black women, as legitimate in their own right and sees Black women's experiences as valid and requiring no additional or outside validation. Standpoint theory[15], which served as the theoretical foundation for the 'Black Women Big Data' project, requires a centering and privileging of Black women's experiences as legitimate topics of study and acknowledges the group knowledge produced through shared lived experiences.

CORPORA AS SOCIO-POLITICAL ENTITIES

An acknowledgement of the politicized nature of knowledge production and legitimacy requires a critical analysis of the corpora creation process within computational analysis generally, and topic modeling specifically. Before there is discussion of how to process data or interpret topics, there must be a corpus created with which to process and interpret. The researcher must identify a source(s) from which she will draw her data. This initial step is ripe with political implications, which include but are not limited to the reification and amplification of the source(s) as legitimate and worthy of study. Questions which consider the types of authors contributing to the source(s), whether the source(s) is informal or formal (e.g. social media or peer-reviewed), how these sources are maintained and funded, etc. all expose the ways in which data can be subjective and provide insight into the political aspects of corpora creation. Because of these limitations, which are structurally embedded within corpora and which are rarely critically interrogated, we argue that researchers should (re)interpret corpora as socio-political entities unto themselves, which are created within, and not distinct from, the realms of the social and political. Indeed, the digital is political. Critical reinterpretation of corpora as socio-political entities allows researchers to expose the covert colorblind logic, which is perpetuated within computational analysis when presenting corpora as apolitical and objective. The digital humanities has the potential to lead a politicized digital revolution which could serve to combat rather than reinforce the erasure of Black women's narratives by embedding within the method the legitimization of Black women's experiences as valid areas of knowledge exploration. This reinterpretation of corpora as socio-political entities unto themselves calls upon researchers to consider computational modeling methods as manifestations of theory. And, in the case of our original study, this would include theory, which exposes spaces of power imbalance and seeks to recreate once uncritical spaces.

COMBATTING ERASURE OF BLACK WOMEN: ISSUES WITH FORMAL SOURCES
FOR CORPORA CREATION

Digital libraries such as HathiTrust and JSTOR are considered formal sources of corpora creation because they are legitimized through formal academic agencies, which adhere to specific standards related to what data is included within collections as well as specific standardized processes through which one gains access to such data. Structural barriers around access within academia are reified in the demographics of the creators/authors of this data. For example, the use of the HathiTrust and JSTOR digital libraries for the 'Black Women Big Data' project yielded few sources/documents written by and about African American women (when compared to the larger corpus), which limited efforts to recover narratives of Black women.

While archival metadata does not include a field identifying an author's race or gender, searching by Library of Congress subject headings can create a list of documents by or about specific population groups. As of June 2015, the

HathiTrust, an archive heavily represented by social science and humanities volumes, holds digitized copies of approximately 13.5 million documents, with 5 million in the public domain. Yet a search for document that include 'African American' in their subject heading returns only 24,149 documents, with only 5,318 accessible for research or reading in the public domain. These low numbers are likely caused by a combination of three factors. First, documents written by African American authors are unevenly prioritized during the digitization process. For example, almost no African American newspapers are available through HathiTrust; however, a handful of magazines or journals associated with important cultural figures such as W.E.B. DuBois' The Crisis are available. Second, copyright currently protects all documents published during or after 1923. As a result, important historical moments that produced large volumes of nationally circulating texts like the Harlem Renaissance or the Civil Rights Movement are closed to computational analysis even if documents related to them have been digitized.[16] Finally, metadata standards and cataloging practices may differ significantly across libraries, especially with respect to older documents cataloged prior to 1923. Because researchers have to rely on metadata to organize and navigate large corpora, there may be a significant number of relevant but essentially 'invisible' documents. While a full text search for key phrases could bypass metadata to locate them, such a search would likely return such a large volume of results that researchers would still need a way to identify these invisible documents in a way that did not rely on metadata records.

When combatting the erasure of Black women from 'big data' corpora, it is important to also understand the socio-historical forces that rendered them erased. After the 1739 Stono slave rebellion in South Carolina, the state became one of the first to ban slaves from learning how to write.[17] Other states followed with similar laws to prevent rebellions and other types of resistance to slavery. Despite these extreme barriers and erasures, some Black women have been able to write, or dictate to others, narratives and poetry about their lived experiences, including Phillis Wheatley, Harriet Jacob, and Harriet Tubman.[18] Later, Black feminists began to more deliberately point out, write about and offer critique.[19] The Combahee River Collective Statement served as a written account of a Black feminist movement which sought to acknowledge the various social positions Black women occupy, as related to race, class, sexuality, etc. and to undo the erasure produced within the white feminist movement.[20] More recent barriers and erasures are seen as Black women enter the academy but often struggle to get their research published in mainstream journals and White feminist journals.[21] Patricia Hill Collins made an important intervention in publishing *Black Feminist Thought: Knowledge, Consciousness, and the Politics of Empowerment,* which captures the ideas and activism of African American women that contribute to the social sciences.[22] Collins highlights work complementary to that of Audre Lorde, Kimberlè Crenshaw, Darlene Clark

Hine, and others and elucidates intersectionality and its usage by academic and activist women[23]. As a result of this outsider within status, Black women have created their own publishing outlets such as publishing houses, journals, poetry lithographs, chapbooks (small books or pamphlets), and posted their stories in New York City train stations.[24] As recently as 2008, Mignon Moore made history when she became the first Black woman to publish in both the American Sociological Review and the American Journal of Sociology. These structural constraints mean that researchers using 'big data' must ask of their corpora the following questions: What type of texts (academic journals, academic books, etc.) are in the corpora and what types of texts may be underrepresented in the corpora (poetry, pamphlets, self-published works, etc.)? Historically, who (e.g., more educated Black women) has generally published in the academic journals that are prominent in the corpora?

THEORY TO METHOD: BLACK FEMINIST READING OF METHODS TO RESCUE BLACK WOMEN NARRATIVES

Incorporating the tenets of Black feminism into computational analysis, scholars, particularly those using 'big data', must pay careful attention to the intersectional nature of oppression that often silences the voices of Black women across race, class, gender, sexuality, etc. When rescuing the narratives of Black women from the silencing digitized terrain, which too often erases them, attention to the social location of Black women is critical. Researchers must acknowledge that Black women's lived experiences are often different from Black men and White women, resulting in different standpoints that should be evident in 'big data' analysis. This also means that it may be more challenging to rescue and recover Black low-income women's voices or Black lesbian, gay, bisexual, transgender, queer and intersex (LGBTQI) voices.

In the 'Black Women Big Data' project, the corpora dated back to 1870, which presented the historical limitations mentioned earlier. Therefore, in an attempt to reclaim Black women's voices, the project team isolated texts that were by and/or about Black women (based on catalog data) and, in the African American tradition of 'call and response', sought to identify whether a structural 'call and response' was present within the data. Indeed, call and response as critical method serves to expose patterns, and encourages the consideration of data as interactive and dynamic rather than static.[25]

In non-digital research, archival recovery projects involve the discovery of a previously unacknowledged and non-canonical text that provides important new insights within academic discourse. These recovered texts may have been overlooked by researchers or librarians, hidden away in a private collection, or simply unavailable to scholars due to a limited number of surviving copies. Scholars might know of their existence by making note of references to them in documents with which they are already familiar. Alternatively, scholars might serendipitously stumble upon these documents if they are in physical proximity to them while studying documents with which they are already aware.

Recovery in a digital environment is a similar process. While scholars could search through a digital collection by hand, file-by-file, as they might a physical archive, digital data sources have already eclipsed the scale of even the largest academic libraries. The key difference between physical and digital materials is that researchers will need to construct a new search procedure that can search a large corpus on their behalf without relying on metadata. Yet much like a physical archive, scholars can study around the edges of the known to discover the previously overlooked. Searching for these invisible documents therefore requires researchers to train machine learning algorithms using a representative sample of known documents. Mimicking the 'call and response' tradition mentioned earlier, Latent Dirichlet allocation (LDA)[26] topic modeling was applied to a representative sample of known African American documents to establish a discursive model of African American writing during a given period. Once researchers were confident in its representativeness, we performed a process called 'inference' to test the word distributions of potentially overlooked documents against those in the representative sample. Currently, digital humanities researchers typically use the MALLET software's implementation of LDA topic modeling to study the discursive make-up and development over time of data sets. In these contexts, MALLET tries to fit every word in every document into a fixed number of patterns provided by the researcher. When performing inference on an already established model, however, MALLET will return empty data vectors full of zeros if a document does not fit any of the patterns found in the representative sample. Non-zero vectors would thus potentially identify recoverable documents by or about African Americans that were not explicitly marked as such by their metadata. Researchers could also use other machine learning techniques, provided they could identify the most salient stylistic or syntactic features of the documents in their representative sample.

Rescue and recovery in large datasets is an ongoing process. After retrieving and studying a set of previously invisible documents, researchers may decide to improve the original model by adding the new documents to the training corpus and re-training the model's parameters. In cases where no documents in a collection have reliable metadata, documents from outside the corpus could be used to generate a model.

COMPLEXITY OF DATA AND CHALLENGES OF RESCUE AND RECOVERY

Even though textual data is usually not considered 'big data' unless it reaches a scale involving millions of documents, corpora composed of documents from different genres and data sources requires carefully constructed, nuanced workflows. Multiple factors contribute to data complexity in such a corpus. Collections that include documents that are of widely varying lengths, from short tracts to journal articles to novels, can have significant effects on popular algorithms that analyze word distribution patterns. Latent Dirichlet allocation (LDA) topic modeling, for example, works more effectively on shorter documents and assumes that documents will be of roughly the same length. Since LDA treats inputs as 'bags of words'[27], an uneven distribution of bag size will affect the generated topics. This can be addressed by 'chunking' documents into consistent lengths.[28] Additionally, some documents may employ conventions that may produce a great deal of statistical noise. Almanacs, gazetteers, and city directories, for example, often contain large sections of text that are presented as lists, tables, or other non-prosal forms. These types of documents have a tendency to strongly contribute to a few specific topics. The research team was able to identify these types of documents by developing a new technique called 'intermediate reading', a method of topic interpretation which utilizes document title lists in a process of reading digitized text that is situated between the close readings associated with traditional research and the distant readings of text associated with topic modeling output.[29] Additional issues can be introduced during the digitization phase including optical character recognition errors, uncommon typographical conventions, and operator error. These issues can result in topics containing what look like misspelt words. Metadata also presents difficulties. Meta data describing documents is often incomplete, with no way to verify or authenticate it other than revisiting the source material and doing additional research. Additionally, the English language inherently provides layers of complexity and redundancy. The filtration of stop words, such as articles, personal pronouns, and prepositions, which do not materially affect the sentence meaning, collapsing of verb tenses via stemming, and combining of word inflections into single canonical forms through lemmatization help reduce some of the complexity and redundancy found in English text.

Finally, large collections digitized from multiple sources may also exhibit uneven quality of optical character recognition. Digitized versions of documents printed by smaller presses using outdated equipment or simply documents that were dirty or damaged at the time of scanning may produce patterns of misspellings, at best, or large passages of garbled prose, at worst. Working with a large, widely varied collection requires solutions that account for these problems without creating new ones.

In addition to those previously mentioned, there are other significant challenges and limitations to using machine learning in recovery. For instance, establishing 'representativeness' is already a difficult task in more traditional archival projects. Digital projects are usually conducted on a much larger scale, making it even more difficult to determine how well a set of documents represents a particular identity or politic. It is therefore important to remember the allure of 'objectivity' that many data scientists present their algorithms with and to resist its rhetoric when theorizing and presenting results.

On a more practical level, the larger a collection the more difficult it becomes for researchers to reliably interpret models and the kinds of documents they might be used to retrieve. Large collections containing different genres (fiction, religious works, government publications, journal articles, etc.) add to the complexity of the corpus. Some documents are possibly irrelevant (almanacs, gazetteers, city directories, etc.) and do not contain much more raw textual data than prose. The stylistic and syntactic conventions that define fiction, religious works, government publications, journal articles, etc. will affect algorithms in different ways. The same techniques that delineate variation between those conventions may not work as well for identifying patterns across them. Reducing a collection of hundreds of thousands of documents down to several dozen topics or clusters still requires that researchers spend hours reading over and interpreting complex, confusing data. In the case of LDA topic modeling, for example, the topic key word groupings may be suggestive of certain concepts, but a closer look at the documents themselves may show that they represent something else entirely. For example, in our experience working with a large, mixed genre collection, fiction often causes LDA to produce at least one topic focused on body parts. In addition, during analysis the project team discovered several topics, which initially seemed irrelevant but upon further analysis were found to be of interest. For example, a topic with 'bird, white, black, red, and fish' among its word list was initially determined to be about nature and wildlife. Upon further review, through the process of 'intermediate reading', the following titles were discovered to have partly comprised this topic: Sprung Sonnet for Dorothy Dandridge by Colleen McElroy; For Black Girls Only by Constantine Taylor; Summerpoem 1986 by Sonia Sanchez; To the Poet Who Happens to Be Black and The Black Poet Who Happens to Be a Woman by Audre Lorde. Through further examination, we discovered that a topic initially believed to be about wildlife actually included documents by and about Black women, suggesting that researchers must be cautious and vigilant when interpreting large corpora across genres.

FUTURE OF DIGITAL HUMANITIES

A major limitation of the 'Black Women Big Data' project was the use of JSTOR and HathiTrust formal databases in efforts to understand the experiences of Black women. There exist informal sources of corpora creation, such as social media, which are ripe with opportunity in combatting this limitation. Because of social media's (more) open digital access and disproportionate usage among people of color, particularly Black women, we are now able to identify sources of information specifically written by, about and for Black women. Digital humanities scholars are well placed to tap into these rich sources of knowledge.

When attempting to rescue and recover the complexity of Black women's lived experiences from erasure, social media blogs and microblogs (i.e. Twitter, Facebook) represent a unique way to interrogate new questions using advances in online technology. These are often spaces where Black women create their identities. This is what the author of 'All the Digital Humanists Are White, All the Nerds Are Men, but Some of Us Are Brave', says is meeting Black women 'where they are'.[30]

Another limitation of a corpus using JSTOR and HathiTrust databases is that the vast majority of its books, articles and volumes come from the United States. An exploration of the study of Black women utilizing database with international sources, such as *Africa Analysis*, *Africa Dialogue Monograph Series*, and *Insight*, would put our topic modeling themes in conversation with Africana Diaspora feminists, thus broadening our Black feminist tenets to include a more complete, international focus. Broadening the corpus to include international sources would also allow for virtual 'border-crossing' across databases, whereby researchers could use models built from one database (i.e. Africana Diaspora feminist database) and apply the model to another (i.e. U.S feminist database). This type of border-crossing would assist researchers in understanding how these databases, which create socio-political corpora, are similar or different, thus exposing another dimension of global power dynamics embedded within knowledge creation and corpora analysis.

Approaching computational analysis from the Black feminist tradition, researchers can use topic modeling not only to 'read' text from the perspective of distant reading of large corpora, but also 'read', or rather, critically interpret these computational methods and processes using the tenets of Black feminism. For example, a widely held position within Black feminism deals with the interconnectedness of identities and oppressions. In this essay, we have made the case for rescue and recovery of Black women's narratives from the past. Consider for a moment the possibilities of topic modeling assisting in a form of time travel, not just backward but also forward.[31] Afrofuturism is an exploration of literary and cultural aesthetic production, which reframes the future within the context of technological advances in order to envision Black futures and address issues affecting people of the African Diaspora.[32] Afrofuturists such as Octavia Butler, Kali Tal and Alondra Nelson have utilized imaginings of the future to provide cultural and disciplinary critiques. For example, Butler utilizes technological imaginings to provide social critique and address African American concerns. Digital humanities can learn from Afrofuturists and use computational technology to not only project Black women forward and possibly decenter westernized views, but also to predict future narratives related to Black women based on current conversations captured and/or current and historical patterns within text.[33] A Black feminist reading of method allows for such conceptualizations.

If researchers can train algorithmic models to identify and replicate patterns in data, we can train models to project forward where or when topics might reappear, perhaps shifting in how they are spoken about but (re)emerging none the less. We may also be able to predict topic shifts, perhaps based on the appearance of other distinct topics, with an understanding that all relationships, even those between words in a corpus and particularly relationships of power and oppression, are interconnected. Under this premise, it is possible to uncover and recover these interconnected patterns within the data. For example, it may be possible to discover an algorithmic thread which connects discussions of lynching during Ida B. Wells' era, state violence against communities of color during the 1960s, and the current Black Lives Matter movement that may allow us to predict when or how future discussions around state-sanctioned violence against communities of color might manifest. Informal data sources may be better equipped for this type of forward projection as they are not bound by the constraints of formal sources (e.g., peer review process), which are slower in bringing contemporary issues to the forefront. More importantly, formal sources are constrained in how they legitimize experiences and knowledge. In this way, topic modeling can serve as a methodological tool of survival for issues affecting Black women. The prospect of projecting Black women forward into the future using computational analysis breathes theoretical and political life into an understudied and intellectually underappreciated social group and connects the (digitized) survival, persistence, and preservation of this group with that of the digital humanities.

END NOTES

[1] T. McPherson, 'Why are the Digital Humanities so white? Or thinking the histories of race and computation', *Debates in the Digital Humanities*, http://dhdebates.gc.cuny.edu/debates/text/29, last accessed 6 November, 2015

[2] McPherson, 'Why are the Digital Humanities so white? Or thinking the histories of race and computation'; A.D. Nieves and M. Jaksch, 'Africa is a country? Digital diasporas, ICTs, and heritage development strategies for social justice', *The Journal of Interactive Technology and Pedagogy*, http://jitp.commons.gc.cuny.edu/africa-is-a-country-digital-diasporas-icts-and-heritage-development-strategies-for-social-justice/, last accessed 6 November, 2015; M.N. Smith, *About: Dickinson electronic archives*, http://www.emilydickinson.org/about, last accessed 6 November, 2015; T. Underwood, *We don't already understand the broad outlines of literary history*, http://tedunderwood.com/2013/02/08/we-dont-already-know-the-broad-outlines-of-literary-history/, last accessed 6 November, 2015.

[3] In terms of Black feminism in the U.S., see B. Smith, *Home girls: a black feminist anthology*, (New Brunswick, 1983); The Combahee River Collective, 'A black feminist statement', in G.T. Hull, P.B. Smith, and B. Smith, eds., *All the women are white, all the Blacks are men, but some of us are brave*, (New York, 1981).; b. hooks, 'Black women shaping feminist theory',

in *Feminist theory: from margin to centre*, (Boston, 1984).; b. hooks, *Ain't I a woman: Black women and feminism*, (Boston 1981).; A. du Cille, 'The occult of true black womanhood: critical demeanor and black feminist studies', *Signs: Journal of Women in Culture and Society*, 19 (3), 591–629.; B. Guy-Shefthall, *Words of fire: an anthology of African-American feminist thought*, (New York, 1995).; S. M. James and A. P.A. Busia, *Theorizing black feminisms: the visionary pragmatism of Black women*, (London, 1993).; E. F. White, *Dark continent of our bodies: black feminism and the politics of respectability*, (Philadelphia, 2001).; H. Carby, 'On the threshold of woman's era: lynching, empire, and sexuality in black feminist theory', in H.L. Gates Jr., ed., *Race, writing and difference* (Chicago, 1983).; b. hooks, *Talking back : thinking feminist, thinking black* (Boston, 1989).

[4] The HathiTrust is a digital library and access platform, which is comprised of volumes from primarily U.S. research institutions and libraries. Half of the collections held within HathiTrust are written in English. See also 'HathiTrust Languages', https://www.hathitrust.org/visualizations_languages, last accessed 6 November, 2015.; JSTOR is a digital library of primarily U.S. based academic journals. See also 'Data for Research: About JSTOR', http://about.jstor.org/service/data-for-research, last accessed 6 November, 2015.

[5] See for example F. Moretti, 'The great slaughterhouse of literature', *MLQ: Modern Literature Quarterly* 61.1 (2000), 207–27. Moretti's essay is one of the most explicit in terms of framing his interest in the canon. He states explicitly that he is not interested in challenging or expanding the canon. Instead, he wants to get a perspective on the literary field 'as a whole' that nonetheless implicitly remains focused around the canon consisting largely of white male authors by incorporating 'rivals' that 'write more or less like canonical authors...but not quite'. Cited here at 207–8.

[6] P.H. Collins, *Black feminist thought: knowledge, consciousness and the politics of empowerment* (New York, 1990).

[7] See A. Koh, '*Addressing archival silence on 19th century colonialism – part 2: creating a nineteenth century 'postcolonial' archive*' Blog entry 4 March 2012 http://www.adelinekoh.org/blog/2012/03/04/addressing-archival-silence-on-19th-century-colonialism-part-2-creating-a-nineteenth-century-postcolonial-archive/ last accessed 31 July 2015.; See also T. McPherson, 'US operating systems at mid-century: the intertwining of race and UNIX', *Race after the Internet* (2012), 21–37.

[8] D. Kim and J. Stommel, *Disrupting the Digital Humanities*, http://disruptingdh.com, last accessed 13 June 2015.

[9] See also C. Sandoval, *Methodology of the oppressed* (Minneapolis, 2000); F. Fanon, *A dying colonialism* (New York, 1959); G. Anzaldua, *Borderlands/la frontera: the new mestizo* (San Francisco, 1987); L. Quinby and D. Hope, *Women confronting the new technologies* (New York, 2001); A. Balsamo, 'The virtual body in cyberspace', *Research in Philosophy and Technology* 13 (1993), 119–39.; A. Balsamo, *Technologies of the gendered body: reading cyborg women* (Durham and London, 1996).; D. Haraway, 1991. 'A cyborg manifesto: science, technology, and socialist-feminism in the late twentieth century', in *Simians, cyborgs and women: the reinvention of nature* (New York, 1991), 149–81.

[10] J.S. Bianco, 'This Digital Humanities which is not one', in M. Gold, ed., *Debates in the Digital Humanities*, (Minneapolis, 2012). Cited here at 97.

[11] P.H. Collins, *Fighting words: Black women and the fight for social justice* (Minneapolis, 1998). Cited here at 277.

[12] B. Agozino, 'Committed objectivity in race, class, gender research', *Quantity and Quality: International Journal of Methodology* 33 (1999), 395–410.

[13] A. Zerai, *Hypermasculinity, state violence, and family well-being in Zimbabwe: an Africana feminist analysis of maternal and child health* (Trenton, 2014). Cited here at 88.

[14] Collins, *Black feminist thought: knowledge, consciousness and the politics of empowerment*.

[15] For an overview of standpoint theory in relation to Black women, see for example, P. H. Collins, 'Learning from the outsider within: the sociological significance of black feminist thought', *Social Problems*, 33 (1986), S14-S32.; P. H. Collins, 'Comment on Hekman's 'truth and method: feminist standpoint theory revisited': where's the power?', *Signs*, 22 (1997), 375–381.; For a general overview of standpoint feminist theory see: S. G. Harding, ed., *The feminist standpoint theory reader: intellectual and political controversies* (New York, 2004).

[16] For additional information related to copyright restrictions for HathiTrust data access and implications for computational research, see 'Copyright' https://www.hathitrust.org/copyright, last accessed 13 November 2015.

[17] B.C. Campbell, *American disasters: 201 calamities that shook the nation* (New York, 2008).

[18] P. Wheatley, *Poems on various subjects, religious and moral* (n.p., 1773).; H. Jacob, *Incidents in the life of a slave girl* (New York, 1861).; S.E. Bradford, *Scenes in the life of Harriet Tubman* (Auburn, 1869).

[19] See G. Yancy 'Feminism and the subtext of whiteness: Black women's experiences as a site of identity formation', *Western Journal of Black Studies*, 24 (2000), 1–2 where he exposes the whiteness of first wave feminism and its false claims of objectivity and discusses how white feminism reifies an 'other' as well as the tension between race and gender as it relates to white feminist claims of fighting for 'women's' issues.

[20] The Combahee River Collective was an organization formed in 1974 as an outgrowth of the National Black Feminist Organization. The group of Black feminists came together for weekly meetings and during a series of retreats in 1977 developed what would become the Combahee River Collective Statement.

[21] A. Hurtado, 'Theory in the flesh: toward an endarkened epistemology', *Qualitative Studies in Education*, 16 (2003), 215–225.

[22] Collins, *Black feminist thought: knowledge, consciousness and the politics of empowerment.*

[23] A. Lorde, *Sister outsider*, (Freedom, CA, 1990).; Kimberlè Crenshaw, 'Demarginalizing the intersection of race and sex: a black feminist critique of antidiscrimination doctrine, feminist theory, and antiracist politics', *Chicago Legal Forum*, (1989), 139–67.; D.C. Hine, E.B. Brown and R. Terborg-Penn, *Black women in the United States: an historical encyclopedia*, (New York, 1993).;

[24] C. Moraga and G. Anzaldúa, *This bridge called my back: writings by radical women of color* (Watertown, 1981).; Hurtado, 'Theory in the flesh: toward an endarkened epistemology'.

[25] The term 'call and response' refers to speech patterns found in African-American oral tradition whereby within a community of speakers, one speaker calls out to a group and the group responds. See M. Sale, 'Call and response as critical method: African-American oral traditions and beloved', *African American Review*, 26 (1992), 41. See also G. Smitherman, *Talkin and testifyin: the language of black America* (Detroit, 1985).

[26] The LDA model assigns each word a probability according to each topic. Words that are more strongly related to a topic will have a higher probability of being generated by the topic. Because each entry in the vector returned by MALLET indicates the probability that the document was generated by that specific topic, we can recover both the overall likelihood that the document is relevant (by marginalizing or adding up the probabilities for all of the specified topics) as well as measuring how much of that relevance is due to each of the topics (by looking at the individual entries and choosing the highest one).

[27] Words are not presented to the model in a sequential order as sentences and paragraphs, as would be encountered with a traditional reading of text. Instead, words are presented as an unordered occurrence counts.

[28] M. Jockers, *Macroanalysis: digital methods and literary history* (Urbana, 2013).

[29] N. M. Brown, R. Mendenhall, M. Black, M. Von Moer, I. Lourenztin and H. Green, 'Methods for using topic models and visualizations with big data to understand Black women's everyday

experiences and standpoints' (unpublished manuscript, University of Illinois at Urbana-Champaign, 2015).

[30] G.Z. Bailey, 'All the digital humanists are white, all the nerds are men, but some of us are brave', *Journal of Digital Humanities,* 1 (2011), 120–121.

[31] X. Wang and A. McCallum, 'Topics over time: a non-Markov continuous-time model of topical trends', *Proceedings of the 12th ACM SIGKDD international conference on knowledge discovery and data mining* (Philadelphia, 2006). The Topics-over-Time (TOT) model extracts time-localized topics from specific events, but also allows for filtering of topics based on co-occurrence with user-specified. It may be possible for models to identify recurrent topics that re-appear in a cyclical fashion.

[32] L. Yaszek, 'An afrofuturist reading of Ralph Ellison's Invisible Man', *Rethinking History,* 9 (2005), 297–313.; M. Bould, 'The ships landed long ago: afrofuturism and black sf', *Science Fiction Studies,* 34 (2007), 177–86.

[33] T. Bristow 'We want the funk: what is afrofuturism to the situation of digital arts in Africa?', *Technoetic Arts: A Journal of Speculative Research,* 10 (2012), 25–32.